MUSIC THEORY

Margaret Richer

teach®
yourself

Dedication

To Lurch, who slept through it all.

Acknowledgements

I would like to thank Helen Hart, Sue Hart, Catherine Coe and other staff at Hodder & Stoughton for their help at various stages in producing this book. Thanks also goes to friends and neighbours who listened attentively to my ideas and gave encouragement. Finally, I thank all the people I have taught throughout the years. Without them, this book would not have been possible.

For UK order enquiries: please contact Bookpoint Ltd, 130 Milton Park, Abingdon, Oxon OX14 4SB. Telephone: +44(0)1235 827720. Fax: +44(0)1235 400454. Lines are open 09.00–18.00, Monday to Saturday, with a 24-hour message answering service. Details about our titles and how to order are available at www.teachyourself.co.uk

For USA order enquiries: please contact McGraw-Hill Customer Services, PO Box 545, Blacklick, OH 43004-0545, USA. Telephone: 1-800-722-4726. Fax: 1-614-755-5645.

For Canada order enquiries: please contact McGraw-Hill Ryerson Ltd, 300 Water St, Whitby, Ontario L1N 9B6, Canada. Telephone: 905 430 5000. Fax: 905 430 5020.

Long renowned as the authoritative source for self-guided learning – with more than 40 million copies sold worldwide – the **teach yourself** series includes over 300 titles in the fields of languages, crafts, hobbies, business, computing and education.

British Library Cataloguing in Publication Data: a catalogue record for this title is available from The British Library.

Library of Congress Catalog Card Number: on file.

First published in UK 2002 by Hodder Arnold, 338 Euston Road, London NW1 3BH.

First published in US 2002 by Contemporary Books, a Division of the McGraw-Hill Companies, 1 Prudential Plaza, 130 East Randolph Street, Chicago, IL 60601 USA.

This edition published 2003.

The **teach yourself** name is a registered trade mark of Hodder Headline Ltd.

Typeset by Dorchester Typesetting Group Ltd. Printed in Great Britain for Hodder Arnold, a division of Hodder Headline, 338 Euston Road, London NW1 3BH, by J. W. Arrowsmith Ltd, Bristol.

Impression number 10 9 8 7 6 5 4

Year   2010 2009 2008 2007 2006 2005

Contents

Introduction

Welcome to *Teach Yourself Music Theory*, a practical approach to learning the mechanics of music. This book is suitable for absolute beginners as well as those with some musical knowledge. Other than a CD player, no special materials are needed to use this book. A music manuscript notebook with printed staff lines would be useful for completing some of the written exercises, although space has been provided in the book itself.

Because it is difficult to learn music theory without applying it, *Teach Yourself Music Theory* takes the fundamentals and presents them with easy-to-follow explanations, examples and exercises. By following a practical approach, the reader will discover through active learning, gaining a clearer understanding based on doing, rather than just memorizing facts.

Learning music theory takes time, practice and repetition. Each new concept is broken into small units followed by exercises reinforcing the material by a variety of written, listening and practical work. Any activity involving the use of the CD is clearly marked by the sign ⓓⓘⓢⓒ . Clear instructions are also given on the CD before an activity begins. Goals to confirm understanding are included at the end of each unit as are any answers to the exercises. Although the exercises themselves do not provide adequate training, they do help in exploring the facts and are an introduction to aural and listening skills. The book is arranged so that each unit builds on what has already been presented, so should be followed in strict order.

Teach Yourself Music Theory contains information that can be applied to all types of music, whether instrumental or vocal, classical or popular. Useful charts, tables and a glossary are found at the back of the book for quick reference. There are also suggestions listed for further study, including use of the internet.

Introducing rhythm

To create any work of art, certain basic elements are needed. In music, these include rhythm, pitch, melody, harmony and tone colour, although each element is not contained in every piece of music. It is difficult to discuss each element individually because they are all dependent on one another when composing music. Rhythm, however, does have more of an identity of its own. In this unit, you will be introduced to the basics of reading, writing and performing rhythm.

In musical terms, rhythm may be broadly defined as anything associated with the duration or length of a sound. It can be completely free, having no basic pulse or divisions to help organize it. Free use of rhythm is found in some primitive music, oriental music and sometimes modern jazz. Most music, however, has a regular pulse, rather like an underlying heartbeat. Musical sounds are written as notes held for different lengths. These notes are combined into patterns forming rhythm.

Note values

This is an example of a music note:
It is the symbol used to show musical sound. ←Stem ←Head

Written music indicates how long a note should sound by its shape. The grouping together of notes of varying lengths creates rhythm. The following table shows the shapes of three notes you will learn in this unit. The British terms, followed by the American, are given. It is helpful to refer to the notes as whole, half and quarter because this shows how their values relate to each other.

Semibreve (whole note) 𝆹	
Minim (half note – lasts half the length of a whole note)	
Crotchet (quarter note – lasts a quarter of a whole note)	
Here's how the note values relate to one another.	

Vertical lines which divide written music into equal segments are called bar-lines. The space between two bar-lines is called a bar or measure. Two vertical lines, a thin followed by a thick one, show the end of a work. Two thin vertical lines indicate the end of a major section of a large work.

When performing, count evenly as though the bar-lines do not exist. There is a very slight accent on the first beat of each bar although this is not shown by notation. Music notes are placed on a staff having five lines and four spaces. The position of the note on the staff shows its pitch; whether it sounds high or low. Because this unit deals only with rhythm, the staff lines will not be used at this point.

Bars and bar-lines

Time signatures

At the beginning of a piece of music, you will find two numbers resembling a fraction. (Note, however, that there is *no* line dividing the two numbers.) This is called the time signature or meter. The top number tells how many beats are in each bar. The bottom number tells the type of note which gets the basic beat. The most common time signature used is $\frac{4}{4}$ time. The top 4 indicates four beats in every bar. The bottom 4 shows that the crotchet (quarter note) gets one beat. Occasionally, a C sign is used for the time signature instead of the numbers. I find it helpful to think of a pie. One whole pie contains two halves and four quarters

4   how many beats in each bar

4   type of note, crotchet (quarter note) gets one beat

Remember, the time signature shows the number of *beats*, not the number of *notes*, per bar. Notes of various lengths are mixed together in a bar of music. They must add up to the proper number of beats required by the time signature.

Exercise 1.1 (Listening)

First look through the examples that follow. On the CD, you will hear each example demonstrated, once with counting, then once without. There are two introductory bars counted before each example to set the pace. Now listen to the CD and see if you are able to follow the notation.

a) $\frac{4}{4}$ 1 2 3 4 | 1 2 3 4 | ♩ ♩ ♩ ♩ | ♩ 𝅗𝅥   𝅗𝅥 | ♩ ♩ ♩ | 𝅝   ‖

b) $\frac{4}{4}$ 1 2 3 4 | 1 2 3 4 | 𝅝 | ♩ 𝅗𝅥   ♩ | ♩ ♩ ♩ ♩ | 𝅗𝅥   ♩ ♩ ‖

c) $\frac{4}{4}$ 1 2 3 4 | 1 2 3 4 | ♩ 𝅗𝅥   ♩ | 𝅝 | ♩ 𝅗𝅥   ♩ | ♩ ♩ ♩ ♩ ‖

These practice tips listed will be helpful in learning to play rhythms correctly.

1   Always look through the music first, noting anything particularly difficult.

2   Count one or two bars before you start to establish the speed.

3   Set the speed slow enough so you will be able to keep a steady pace.

4   When you are clapping a rhythm, keep your hands together to indicate you are holding a note of a longer value.

5   If you have problems keeping an even pace, try using a metronome. These are available as a wind-up instrument which ticks or electric models with a flashing light. The beats on an electric keyboard may also be used.

6   Instead of clapping, exercises may also be practised at a keyboard. Using one finger, select one key and play the rhythm. Remember to hold notes for their full value.

7   Singers might pick a sound such as 'la' and sing the rhythm on one pitch.

Exercise 1.2 (Practical)

Here are some rhythms for you to clap. Before turning on the CD, look through the exercises to make sure you have a general understanding of the material. Each exercise has two bars of count before you begin clapping. The correct rhythm will be demonstrated immediately after your performance.

a) $\frac{4}{4}$ 1 2 3 4 | 1 2 3 4 | ♩♩♩♩ | ♩♩♩ | ♩♩♩ | 𝅗𝅥 ‖

b) $\frac{4}{4}$ 1 2 3 4 | 1 2 3 4 | 𝅗𝅥 ♩♩ | ♩♩♩♩ | ♩♩ | ♩♩♩ 𝅗𝅥 ‖

c) $\frac{4}{4}$ 1 2 3 4 | 1 2 3 4 | ♩♩ 𝅗𝅥 | ♩♩ 𝅗𝅥 | 𝅗𝅥 | ♩♩♩ | ♩♩♩ 𝅗𝅥 ‖

Notation

A stem may either go up or down from the note head. If the stem goes up, it is placed on the right. If the stem goes down, it is placed on the left. More will be mentioned about notation of stems in later units.

Examples of stems   ♩ ♩

Spacing of the notes in the bar is important. The following examples show how proper spacing helps in reading music notation. Study the first bar of example a). The minim (half note) takes up twice as much space as the two crotchets (quarter notes). The relationship is expressed visually.

a) $\frac{4}{4}$ ♩♩ 𝅗𝅥 | 𝅗𝅥 𝅗𝅥 | 𝅗𝅥 ♩♩ | 𝅝 ‖

Example b) is an example of poor spacing. There are the correct number of beats in each bar, but the notes are incorrectly spaced. The first and second crotchets (quarter notes) are placed so that it appears they take up most of the first bar when actually they only occupy the first two beats. The two minims in the second bar should be evenly spaced. In the last bar, the semibreve should be placed at the beginning of the bar because it is played on the first beat and held through the rest of the bar.

b) $\frac{4}{4}$ ♩ ♩ 𝅗𝅥 | 𝅗𝅥 𝅗𝅥 | 𝅗𝅥 ♩♩ | 𝅝 ‖

Exercise 1.3 (Written)

The following are examples of rhythms written in the time signature of $\frac{4}{4}$. Each is four bars long but each bar is incorrect in some way. Correct each exercise in the space below it. You may need to add stems, fill in the heads of the notes or add some notes. There may be more than one correct solution to each. The spacing gives some clues. I've completed the first one for you. The answers are at the end of this unit.

a)

Correct
Version

b)

Correct
Version

c)

Correct
Version

For further practice, try clapping your completed written work. Remember to follow the practice tips.

Exercise 1.4 (Practical)

It is important to be able to hear a rhythm and write it down. The following exercises will help you develop the skill by using rhythm dictation. A 'skeleton' of six bars follows. The first two are for establishing the beat and should be left blank. The following four bars are for writing down the rhythm you hear on the CD. The rhythm will be repeated five times. On each repeat, you should be able to add notes until you have written down the entire four bars.

$\frac{4}{4}$ 1 2 3 4 | 1 2 3 4 | | | | ‖

Time signature of $\frac{2}{4}$

In the time signature of $\frac{2}{4}$ there are two beats in each bar. The crotchet (quarter note) still gets one beat. There is an accent on the first beat of each bar, followed by a weaker second beat. Think of marching: left right, left right, left right . . . the left foot is heavier! Study the example which shows four bars written in $\frac{2}{4}$ time.

strong   weak

music theory

Exercise 1.5 (Written)

Correct the following exercises by adding notes, stems or filling in the heads of the notes.

a)  $\frac{2}{4}$ 𝅗𝅥 𝅗𝅥 | 𝅘𝅥 𝅗𝅥 | 𝅘𝅥 𝅗𝅥 | 𝅝 ‖

Correct
Version $\frac{2}{4}$

b)  $\frac{2}{4}$ 𝅗𝅥 𝅝 | 𝅗𝅥 𝅗𝅥 | 𝅝 | 𝅘𝅥 ‖

Correct
Version $\frac{2}{4}$

c)  $\frac{2}{4}$ 𝅘𝅥 | 𝅝 | 𝅗𝅥 𝅝 | 𝅗𝅥 ‖

Correct
Version $\frac{2}{4}$

� COMPACT disc Exercise 1.6 (Practical)

Here are some rhythms for you to clap. There are two bars of count before you begin. The correct rhythm is performed immediately after your clapping.

a) $\frac{2}{4}$ 1 2 | 1 2 | 𝅘𝅥 𝅘𝅥 | 𝅗𝅥 | 𝅗𝅥 | 𝅘𝅥 𝅘𝅥 | 𝅗𝅥 | 𝅗𝅥 | 𝅘𝅥 𝅘𝅥 | 𝅗𝅥 ‖

b) $\frac{2}{4}$ 1 2 | 1 2 | 𝅘𝅥 𝅘𝅥 | 𝅘𝅥 𝅘𝅥 | 𝅗𝅥 | 𝅘𝅥 𝅘𝅥 | 𝅘𝅥 𝅘𝅥 | 𝅗𝅥 | 𝅘𝅥 𝅘𝅥 | 𝅗𝅥 ‖

Rests

There is a corresponding symbol for each note value that means you do not play a sound. There is silence - you are resting! The symbol is called a rest and is used instead of the note.

𝄽 = 𝅘𝅥   ▬ = 𝅗𝅥   ▬ = 𝅝

(sits on a line when written on the staff)

(hangs down from a line when written on the staff)

Here is an example using rests. If an entire bar is silent, use the semibreve rest no matter what time signature is used.

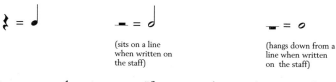

$\frac{4}{4}$ 𝅘𝅥 𝅘𝅥 𝅘𝅥 𝄽 | 𝅗𝅥 ▬ | ▬ | 𝅘𝅥 𝄽 𝅘𝅥 𝄽 ‖

Try drawing a few crotchet (quarter note) rests. You will produce a reasonable rest by first drawing an 'M' on its side, then adding a 'c' to the bottom.

When clapping rhythms, keep your hands together to indicate holding a note, but take your hands apart when counting a rest. On the keyboard, lift your finger to observe the rest. If singing, don't hold the sound through the rest. Observing silence is important. It adds interest to music. Clap the next two examples. The first one is quite boring. The second is much more interesting. What a difference six rests can make!

a)

b)

Exercise 1.7 (Written)
Complete the exercises by adding one rest where the 'R' appears.

a)

b)

Tempo

Tempo is the speed at which music is played. Rhythm refers to the way notes of different lengths are grouped into patterns. A rhythm may be played quickly or slowly. The rhythm itself never changes, but the speed can. In the four bars that follow, the rhythm stays the same whether it is performed slowly or quickly. Try clapping it at different speeds.

Tempo markings are found at the beginning of a piece of music. Sometimes the marking is in English. Italian, however, is the international musical language, so many terms are given in Italian.

Here are a few terms relating to tempo. There is a list of Italian terms in the glossary at the end of the book:

allegro = fast

largo = slow

presto = very fast

andante = walking pace

disc Exercise 1.8 (Practical)

The following rhythms are written in two parts. They may be performed by two people or two groups. The note stems go upwards in the top part while the lower part has stems going downward. This is done purely to help separate the two parts. Notice how important the spacing is when writing for more than one part. The notes need to line up vertically. Two-part exercises are also suitable for individual practice. One hand should tap the top part while the other hand taps the bottom.

On the CD, two bars of introductory count are given. For the first exercise, the bottom line is recorded and the student should clap the top. For the second exercise, the top line is recorded and the student claps the bottom. This gives you practice playing with someone else. When playing with others, you must keep going, even if you make a mistake. No one else is going to stop and wait for you!

disc Exercise 1.9 (Practical)

This final exercise provides listening practice in the form of leader/follower. On the CD you will hear a short rhythm followed by a silence. Listen closely to the rhythm given by the 'leader' and then clap it immediately in the following silence. The rhythms vary in length. Don't worry if you can't do them all. Try to keep going. There is not time to stop and correct yourself. There will be two bars of count at the beginning before the 'leader' starts.

GOALS

Before moving on, make sure you know the following:

1 The names and note values of o 𝅗𝅥 𝅘𝅥. .

2 What the top and bottom numbers of the time signatures indicate.

3 The function of rests.

4 Practice tips for performing rhythms.

5 Importance of correct musical notation, including spacing between notes.

6 The difference between tempo and rhythm.

Answers

Exercise 1.3

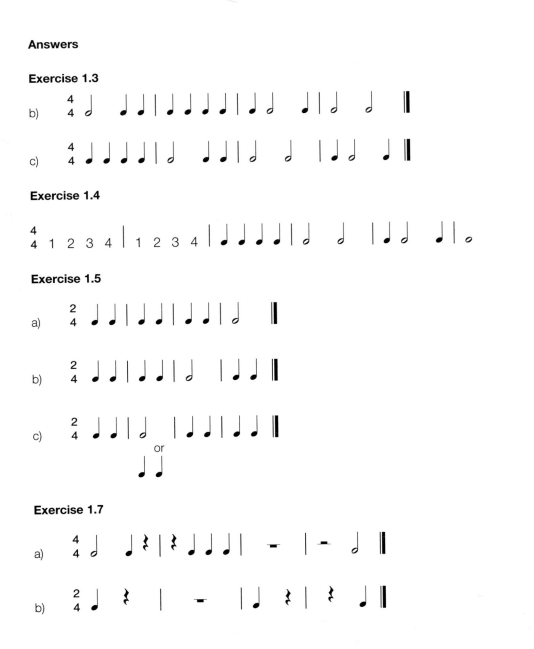

Exercise 1.4

Exercise 1.5

Exercise 1.7

2

Pitch

In this unit, we will leave rhythm for the moment and start exploring the element of pitch. In music theory, the word 'pitch' is used to indicate the lowness or highness of a sound. Technically, pitch is determined by the number of vibrations per second or frequency of a sound. The faster the vibration, the higher the pitch. Low sounds, therefore, have a slow frequency. Musical pitches are given letter-names based on the first seven letters of the alphabet and are written as notes on a staff. Before going any further, let's stop and concentrate on learning more about high and low pitch by using the keyboard as a means of demonstration.

The keyboard and musical alphabet

There are seven letters used in music, called the musical alphabet. They are A, B, C, D, E, F and G. The keyboard diagram (Figure 2.1) shows how the seven letter-names are arranged and repeated up and down the keys of the keyboard. Moving upwards (to the right) the sounds become higher in pitch and moving downwards (to the left) the sounds become lower in pitch.

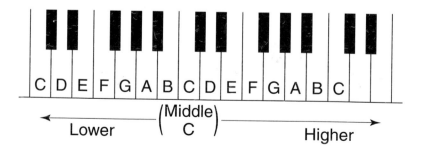

■ Figure 2.1

Exercise 2.1 (Practical)

On the CD, you will first hear a demonstration of pitches moving upwards (higher) from middle C, then moving lower. You will then hear a second series of pitches for you to identity as high or low. Listen carefully to each sound as it is played. Write down whether you think it is higher in pitch or lower than the previous sound. An example will be given on the CD before you start the exercise. H L H H H L H

Groupings of keys

It is important to understand fully the arrangement of the keyboard, as this will be an aid in learning about the different aspects of music theory presented in this book. Take a few minutes to study the picture of the keyboard. You will find there are both white and black keys. The black keys are arranged in groups of two and three. I like to refer to these groups as 'landmarks'. They are helpful in locating the white keys and generally finding your way around the keyboard. Always try to be aware of how the keys relate to one another. Notice, for example, how D is located in the middle of the two black keys. One key up (higher) from D is E. When moving upwards, say the musical alphabet forwards. One key down (lower) from D is C. When moving downwards, the alphabet is backwards.

Exercise 2.2 (Practical)

Using the keyboard diagram, practise locating the following:

a)   All the groups of two black keys, up and down the keyboard.

b)   Point to all the Ds, then all the Es.

c)   Locate all the groups of three black keys.

d)   Find all the Fs. (This is the white key located just to the left of the three black keys.)

e)   Find all the Gs, As and Bs.

Exercise 2.3 (Practical)

This exercise is designed to help you develop speed in finding your way around the keyboard. You will be asked to locate various keys on your diagram. There will be a space between each instruction to give you ample time to find what you are looking for.

The staff

Music notes are written on a staff consisting of five lines and the four spaces between the lines. The plural of staff is staves. The placement of the note shows its pitch; whether its sound is high or low. A note may be written with a line running through it and is then called a 'line' note. Notes may also be placed in the spaces between the lines. These are 'space' notes. Be sure to remember that 'notes' are written on the staff. 'Keys' are found on the keyboard. You do not play the 'notes' of a keyboard . . . you play the 'keys'.

Examples of line notes

Examples of space notes

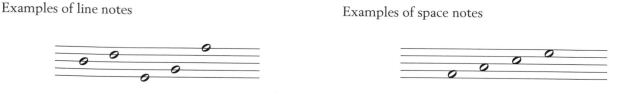

◼ Figure 2.2

◼ Figure 2.3

A clef sign is found at the beginning of each staff. The treble clef, also called the G clef, curls around the second line. A note with the second line running through it is the pitch of G. This is a good landmark when reading music. Try drawing a few treble clefs. It is easiest to start with the vertical line followed by the top curve. The final curl should be around the second line.

◼ Figure 2.4

Middle C

The musical staff did not always consist of just five lines and four spaces. As early music evolved, more lines were added until there were 11. This became difficult to read, so the line in the middle was removed. It now appears as a short line called a leger or ledger line. This line is used for the note of middle C. Piano music is written using two staves joined together by a brace. This is called the grand staff. In general, the notes for the right hand are written on the upper staff, using the treble clef. The notes for the left hand are written on the lower staff using the bass clef.

Staff with 11 lines

◼ Figure 2.5

Middle C may be written in two ways. When it is to be played by the right hand, it appears nearer the upper staff as shown in the following example. If middle C is to be played by the left hand, it appears nearer the bass clef.

Grand staff showing positions of middle C

■ Figure 2.6

Beginning to read notes in treble and bass clef

Notes in the treble clef

You will now start learning to recognize the different pitches as they are written as notes on the staff. Only a few notes will be introduced at one time to make learning easier. Here are the first five notes of the treble clef, starting with middle C. The lowest line, E, is called the first line and the first space is F. Notice that the space beneath the staff created by the leger line middle C and the first line E is used to place the note, D.

Five notes in treble clef

■ Figure 2.7

When reading music, the relationship in movement between the notes is important. Notice whether a note moves up or down and by step or skip. A step is when movement is to a note directly above or below the previous one. An example is E followed by F, a line note moving to a space note. If a line note moves to another line note, there has obviously been a skip. Skips may be small (C moving up to E) or larger (C moving up to G).

Exercise 2.4 (Written)

Here is a series of notes for you to identify by name. Write the letter-names under each semibreve (whole note). Don't worry about adding stems or filling in the note heads. This exercise is purely for practice in reading pitches and does not involve rhythms.

■ Figure 2.8

Now write your own series, then go back and write the names under each one.

■ Figure 2.9

Notes in the bass clef

Study the five notes written here in bass clef.

Five notes in bass clef

■ Figure 2.10

The bass clef is also called the F clef. Two dots are placed on each side of the fourth line, F. You will probably find it more difficult to remember these new notes because they do not move in a straightforward alphabetical order. Establishing landmarks will help you in your music reading. Middle C is a good landmark as it is easy to recognize. Remembering that the two dots surround the F line is also helpful.

Exercise 2.5 (Written)
Write the names underneath each of the semibreves (whole notes).

f a g c b g b f g

Figure 2.11

Write your own series, then go back and add the name under each.

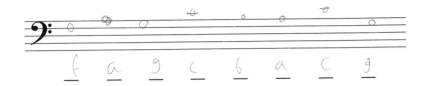

f a g c b a c g

■ Figure 2.12

⬚COMPACT disc Exercise 2.6 (Practical)
Remembering the names of the notes takes time and repetition. This exercise provides further practice in learning the notes of the staff. On the CD, you will hear the names of notes given. Write each one down on the following staff, making sure you use the correct clef. The answers are given at the end of the unit.

■ Figure 2.13

GOALS

1 Define 'pitch'.

2 Know the letters used in the musical alphabet.

3 Know the arrangement of the keys on the keyboard and be able to locate them quickly.

4 Read and write the notes of middle C, D, E, F, G in treble clef.

5 Read and write the notes of F, G, A, B, middle C in the bass clef.

6 The importance of 'landmarks' and relationships of movement of notes (skips, steps) as useful aids in reading music.

Answers

Exercise 2.4

C F G E F D G F D

Exercise 2.5

F A G C B G B F G

Exercise 2.6

■ Figure 2.14

Melody

In unit 1, you learned how rhythms are formed by using various note values. Unit 2 introduced pitches, showing their location on the keyboard and how they are written on the staff. You are now ready to study how rhythm and pitch are combined to form a melody.

Combining rhythm and pitch

A melody consists of an organized series of different pitches. They are given time values and arranged in a time signature. This is demonstrated in the two examples that follow. Example a) is just a long series of various notes, all written as semibreves (whole notes). In example b), the pitches have been divided into bars, given note values and a time signature. Even before listening to the examples, the second series of notes seems visually to make more sense than a).

■ Figure 3.1

◖ⵀⵙ◗ **Exercise 3.1 (Listening)**
Following the musical notation, listen to the two examples, noticing how the series of pitches was turned into a melody.

Analysing melodies

Before you will be able to write an interesting melodic line, it is necessary to know more about the relationship between rhythm and pitch and how they work together when combined into melodies. To do this, some samples will be analysed in detail.

Exercise 3.2 (Written work)
Two short melodies follow. They are each eight bars in length and use the notes you have already learned in the treble clef, middle C, D, E, F, G. Study each of the melodies, beginning with saying the names of the notes. Next, notice the directions the notes move. Do they move in steps or skips? Are there repetitions of small melodic patterns? Jot down your ideas and compare them with mine found at the end of the unit.

■ Figure 3.2

◖ⵀⵙ◗ **Exercise 3.3 (Listening)**
Listen to each melody in Exercise 3.2 as it is played on the CD. Try to follow the musical notation. Two bars of introduction are played before the melody begins. A background accompaniment is played with the melody to add interest.

Creating rhythms

In your analysis of the previous music, you should have noticed patterns in both the rhythm and pitch. Although a creative activity, music is not just a collection of rhythms and pitches picked at random. Even a short piece of music needs to be carefully planned. In this section, you will begin composing your own music, starting with rhythm.

Rhythms need to be interesting, but also need to be held together by a certain amount of repetition. The next exercise contains the first two bars of a four-bar rhythm. There are various ways to complete the last two bars.

The most obvious way would be to use an exact repeat of the rhythms used in the first two bars. I've composed a few other solutions. Listen to them on the CD.

Exercise 3.4 (Listening)

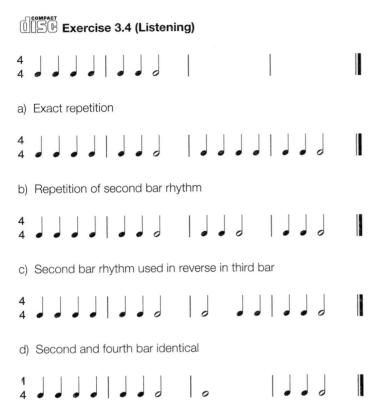

a) Exact repetition

b) Repetition of second bar rhythm

c) Second bar rhythm used in reverse in third bar

d) Second and fourth bar identical

Exercise 3.5 (Written and practical)

The first two bars have been completed in the examples that follow. Compose the final two bars for each one, then clap your completed rhythms.

Phrases

Just as written words have punctuation marks such as commas to help structure a sentence, music also uses a type of punctuation. The phrase is similar to a line of writing and is several bars long. In simple music, a phrase is usually two or four bars in length, but there is no set rule about how long a phrase should last. Phrases group together bars which contain a musical thought. They are notated by a long, curved line starting from the first note and ending at the last note of the phrase.

In example a) that follows, I have written four bars containing two phrases of two bars each. The first two bars have been given, but the last two need to be completed with notes in the treble clef of middle C, D, E, F and G. Examples b) and c) show two different solutions. In b), the first and third bars are the same, both in rhythm and pitch. Bars two and four use the same rhythm but different notes. The repetition of similar patterns help hold the melody together. Think of the first two bars as a question and the last two as the answer. Example c) shows music which does not use repetition or patterns, either in rhythm or pitch. The melody seems to wander without direction, making it harder to remember, once heard. There is no variety in the rhythm until the final bar and the listener is left up in the air.

 Figure 3.3

Exercise 3.6 (Listening)

Turn on the CD and listen to the examples. Notice how example b) is much better balanced and more musical than c).

Exercise 3. 7 (Written)

Practise composing answering phrases to these exercises. You have been given the first two bars for each. Be sure to use patterns and repetitions. Use only the notes of middle C, D, E, F and G in the treble clef. Put all the stems upwards and remember to use proper spacing between the notes.

■ Figure 3.4

What makes a good melody?

A good melodic line has a sense of direction called a melodic curve. It should fit the mood of the music and help express the meaning of any words present. There are different ways of writing a melody with a feeling of direction. One way is to start at its lowest notes and move upward to the highest point. The opposite of this is to start high and work downwards. Other melodies might start low, move to a high point and return to end low. The opposite of this is to start high, reach a low point and return for a high ending. Study the diagrams of these four different melodic curves shown.

a)   Starting low and ending high

b)   Starting high and ending low

c)   Starting low, reaching a high point then ending low

d)   Starting high, reaching a low point and ending high

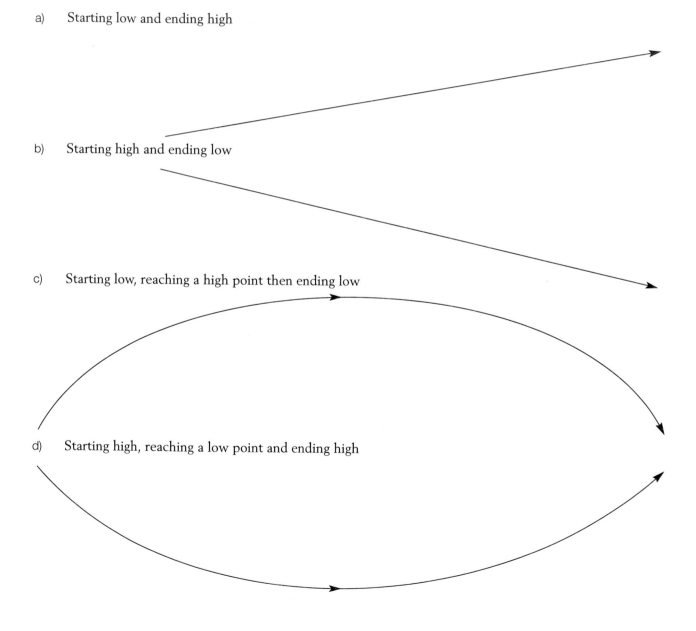

⌐COMPACT⌐ diSC Exercise 3.8 (Practical)

The following exercises will help in developing your aural and listening skills. There will be a demonstration before each exercise.

a) On the CD you will hear a series of pitches. After each pitch there will be a pause for you to sing the pitch. Use 'la' or any sound you feel comfortable singing.

b) You will hear several different groups of three pitches. After hearing each group of three, there will be a pause for you to sing the three pitches you have just heard.

c) The final exercise uses rhythm only. You will hear a short rhythm. Immediately following the rhythm, there is a gap for you to clap an answering rhythm. What your answer consists of is entirely up to you!

GOALS

1 Analyse music, understanding the importance of repetition and patterns.

2 Compose short answering rhythms and melodies.

3 Define 'phrase'.

4 List four types of melodic curve.

5 Sing given pitches accurately.

6 Clap an answering rhythm to a given rhythm.

Answers

Exercise 3.2

a) First bar moves upwards in steps.
   First and third bars are the same.

   Rhythm uses a mixture of o, ♩, ♪ notes.

b) Most of the melody is based on a small skip followed by a step.
   Bars 1 and 2 are the same as 5 and 6.

   Rhythm uses ♩ and ♪ notes.

4

More about pitch

In this unit, the names of the notes for the rest of the staff, both treble and bass clef, are presented. It is important to learn to recognize these because much of the future work is based on being able to read notation quickly and accurately. The written exercises and listening will help you in this learning by repetition and reinforcement. The later part of the unit deals with notation of stems, leger lines and clefs other than treble and bass.

The octave

The treble clef in the following example shows the five notes you have already learned. Added to these are three new ones – A, B, C. The higher C is one octave above middle C. An octave is the repetition of the letter-name of a note. The octave note may be either higher or lower. The seven letter-names of the musical alphabet (the white keys on the keyboard) plus the repeated letter-name make the octave.

Treble clef showing the notes in the C octave

■ Figure 4.1

Study the bass clef now. It also includes three new notes – E, D, C. The lower C is an octave below middle C. It may be helpful to locate the octave and new notes on the keyboard diagram in Unit 2.

C　B　A　G　F　E　D　C

▨ Figure 4.2

Exercise 4.1 (Written)

This written work will give further practice in learning the notes you have studied so far. For the exercise, you need to write the letter-names under each of the notes. Use semibreves (whole notes) because this work deals with pitch only, not rhythm. Remember to think about how the notes move in relation to each other and your landmarks.

a) C　g　f　b　a　c　d♯　f　e　c　g

b) G　C　D　f　c　e　a　b　c　g　f

▨ Figure 4.3

For more practice, you should write your own series of notes and identify them as you have just done.

■ Figure 4.4

■ Figure 4.5

3rd
2nd
3rd
2nd
3rd

octave
3rd
2nd

◎ **disc** Exercise 4.2 (Practical)

This exercise provides a chance to hear what you have been reading and writing about. It is designed to give listening practice in distinguishing the difference in sound between steps, skips and the octave. The step, one note moving to the next directly above or below it, is called a second. Examples are C up to D, E up to F or E down to D. A small skip, leaving one note in between, is a third. Examples include C up to E, D up to F or G down to E. Before starting your listening, locate these examples on the keyboard diagram. Don't worry about the black keys for the present.

   When listening to the demonstration on the CD, notice that the second has a dissonant, rather harsh sound, but the third is consonant and more pleasing to the ear. The octave is easier to recognize as it contains a much larger skip. For the listening exercise which follows the demonstration, you will hear a series of pitches played in pairs, first sounded separately and then together. Each pair will be repeated three times before moving on to the next. You need to indentify each pair as a second, third or octave. Jot down your answers and check them at the end of the unit.

Completing the notes on the staff

The rest of the notes for treble and bass clef come next. Notice that a line note becomes a space note in the next octave and a space note becomes a line note. Exercise 4.3 will help you learn them.

All the notes on the staff

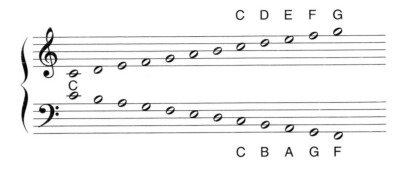

C D E F G

C B A G F

■ Figure 4.6

Exercise 4.3 (Written)

Fill in the names of the pitches. Only the new notes just presented are used but treble and bass clef are both used.

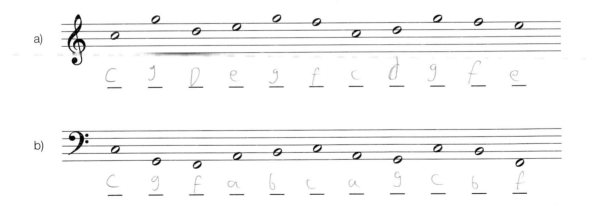

a) C d D e g f c d g f e

b) C g f a b c a g c b f

■ Figure 4.7

music theory

⊙COMPACT disc Exercise 4.4 (Practical)

This exercise uses dictation to provide more practice in developing speed in reading music. On the CD you will hear descriptions of pitches to write on the staff. The first series will be for the treble clef, followed by a series for bass. Answers are at the end of the unit.

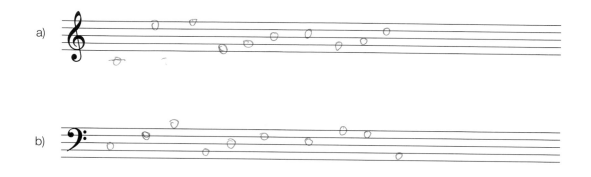

■ Figure 4.8

Notation of stems

Look through the examples that follow and notice the directions of the stems. Some go upwards, while others are downwards. The general rule in music notation is that for any note with the head below the third line, the stem goes upwards. Any note above the third line, the stem goes downwards. If a note is on the third line, the stem may be placed in either direction to fit into the context. Writing stems in the correct direction keeps the music tidy and easy to read. Compare the two examples to see the difference!

■ Figure 4.9

Incorrect

■ Figure 4.10

Leger (ledger) lines

Short lines drawn above or below the staff for notes which are pitched higher or lower are called leger (ledger) lines. Added lines do continue but become increasingly difficult to read.

Staff showing leger lines

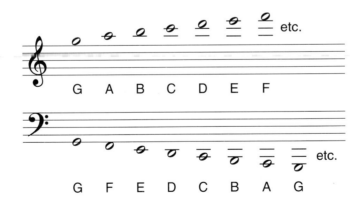

G   A   B   C   D   E   F   etc.

G   F   E   D   C   B   A   G   etc.

■ Figure 4.11

Some notes may appear in both clefs written as leger lines. This happens particularly in piano/keyboard music. The example that follows shows a short piece of piano music written in two different ways. The first is for left hand only in bass clef, followed by the second for right hand in treble clef.

■ Figure 4.12

 Exercise 4.5 (Listening)

Study the pieces in the last two examples, making sure you understand the use of leger lines. Follow the written music while it is played on the CD. You will hear that both tunes sound exactly the same although they are notated differently.

Octave sign – 8va

Pitches may be written an octave lower or higher than they are meant actually to sound. This is done to make them easier to read by avoiding difficult leger lines. The octave sign, 8va, is marked over or under these notes. If it is written above, the notes will sound an octave higher. If written below, the notes will sound an octave lower.

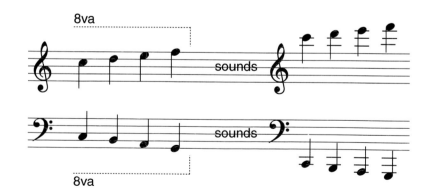

■ Figure 4.13

Other clefs

Besides the treble and bass clefs, there are other less commonly used clefs found in some music. The C clef, written 𝄡, is a moveable clef. This means that it can be placed in any position on the staff to mark a new location for middle C. When the C clef is on the middle line, it is called the alto clef and when on the fourth line, it is called the tenor clef. Alto and tenor clefs are used mainly for music written for certain instruments such as viola, cello, bassoon and sometimes trombone.

Examples of alto and tenor clefs

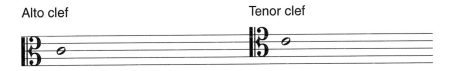

Alto clef   Tenor clef

■ Figure 4.14

Exercise 4.6 (Written)
Name the pitches below in alto and tenor clefs.

a)

b)

■ Figure 4.15

GOALS

1 Define the term 'octave'.

2 Be able to read all the notes in treble and bass clefs.

3 Distinguish the difference in sound when hearing a step, skip and octave.

4 Understand the use of leger lines and the octave sign, 8va.

5 Understand the placement of pitches in alto and tenor clefs.

Answers

Exercise 4.1

a) 𝄞   C G F B A C D F E C G
(middle above first C)

b) 𝄢   G C D F C E A B C G F
(middle above the second C)

Exercise 4.2

2　　3　　8　　3　　2　　8　　8　　3　　2

Exercise 4.3

a) 𝄞   C G D E G F C D G F E

b) 𝄢   C G F A B C A G C B F

Exercise 4.4

■ Figure 4.16

Exercise 4.6

a)   C   E   F   G   F   B

b)   C   G   A   E   F   A

5

More about rhythm

For the moment, let's leave pitch and melody and return to learning more about rhythm. This unit introduces both new time signatures and new note values. There is a section explaining the time signature of $\frac{3}{4}$ and one on dotted notes and ties. Later parts of the unit deal with other note values and less common time signatures. Demonstration, written and practical work are included to help in the learning process.

$\frac{3}{4}$ time

In the time signature of $\frac{3}{4}$, there are three beats in each bar. As in $\frac{2}{4}$ and $\frac{4}{4}$ time, the crotchet (quarter note) gets one beat. $\frac{3}{4}$ time is also known as waltz time. Another dance, the minuet, is also written in $\frac{3}{4}$. Study the following example. It shows that the first beat of each bar receives a slight accent.

strong   weak   weak

Exercise 5.1 (Listening)

On the CD you will hear some examples using $\frac{3}{4}$ time. They will be played at various speeds. Listen for the strong first beat of each bar.

Dotted notes

Dotted notes are often found in $\frac{3}{4}$ time. A small dot placed after a note adds to it half the original value. A minim (half note) which lasts for two beats will be worth three beats when dotted. Rests may also be dotted. A dotted minim (half note) rest lasts for three beats.

Examples of dotted notes and rests

Tied notes

When a note is carried over into the following bar, a curved line called a tie is used. This makes the value of the original note longer because it is joined or tied to the next bar. The curved line is written between the note heads, not the stems. A tie has to be between two notes of the same pitch.

Example showing a tied note

There is no limit on the length of a tie.

Exercise 5.2 (Practical)

The following exercises are in ¾ time and are designed to give practical experience by clapping the rhythms. They include rests, dotted notes and ties. When clapping the exercises, keep your hands together to indicate a note is being held. On the CD you will hear two bars of count before you begin to clap. The correct rhythm will be played directly after your performance. Remember to look through the exercises before turning on the CD.

a)

b)

c)

Exercise 5.3 (Written)

Add bar-lines to the following:

a)

b)

c)

Try composing an eight-bar rhythm of your own. Use dotted notes, ties and rests to make it interesting. Clap your completed rhythm, using a speed you are able to keep steady.

3
4 | | | | | | | ‖

Quavers (eighth notes)

You have seen how in $\frac{2}{4}$, $\frac{3}{4}$, and $\frac{4}{4}$ time the crotchet (quarter note) receives one beat. The quaver (eighth note), however, only lasts for half of one beat in these time signatures, so it becomes necessary to divide each beat into parts smaller than one. Before going any further into counting quavers, let's study how they are written. Quavers are written individually with an added tail to the stem. The tail is always added on the right side. They are also joined together by a beam. If there are several quavers (eighth notes) in a row, it is easier to read them if they are grouped together.

Examples of quavers

Sometimes, there may be groups of four or more quavers beamed together. In $\frac{4}{4}$ time, they should never be beamed across the middle of the bar, as there needs to be a clear indication of where the third beat starts.

Wrong   Correct

The quaver (eighth note) also has a rest written as ϙ.

Counting quavers

There are two quavers (eighth notes) to every crotchet (quarter note) beat, making the quaver worth half a beat. When first learning to count these, it is best to say 'and' between the beats. This helps you place the quaver (eighth note) evenly between the beats. It may be helpful to count 'and' continuously throughout each bar to keep a steady beat. The quavers (eighth notes) will easily fall into place when they occur.

4
4

1 & 2 & 3 & 4 &   1 & 2 & 3 & 4 &

Exercise 5.4 (Practical)

Look through the exercises that follow. They use quavers, rests and ties. The first one will be demonstrated for you, with two bars of introductory count. Try clapping the rest of the exercises. You will hear the correct rhythm played directly after the space left for your performance. Remember to check the time signatures!

Dotted crotchets

A dot placed after a crotchet (quarter note) adds to it half its original value which equals a quaver (eighth note). The dotted crotchet therefore lasts for one and a half counts.

Exercise 5.5 (Listening)

Listen to the three examples on the CD. They will be played once with counting followed by once without.

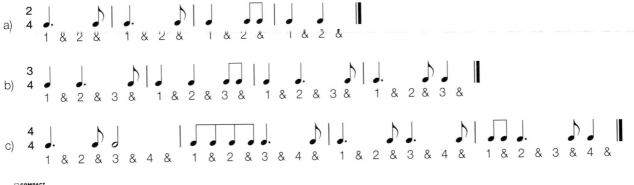

Exercise 5.6 (Practical)

In this exercise, you will hear a backing track for the Cuban dance known as the ChaCha. You are going to join in by clapping a rhythm called the clave. Before turning on the CD, practice the clave rhythm.

Semiquavers (sixteenth notes)

When you previously studied quavers (eighth notes), it was explained that its value was less than one beat. Notes with values shorter than quavers (eighth notes) are sometimes used. A semiquaver (sixteenth note) lasts only half as long as a quaver (eighth note). The next examples show how semiquavers (sixteenth notes) are written and counted. You may find it helpful to count each semiquaver as shown here.

Examples of semiquavers

Semiquavers (sixteenth notes) may also be mixed and joined to notes of other values. Study the examples that follow which show the dotted quaver (eighth note) joined to a semiquaver (sixteenth note). The dotted quaver is equal to three semiquavers.

Exercise 5.7 (Practical)
Try clapping these last three rhythms, keeping your clapping even and steady.

Demisemiquaver (thirty-second note)

There is one other note value which should be mentioned, the demisemiquaver (thirty-second note). It lasts only half as long as the semiquaver (sixteenth note). You will not find demisemiquavers used very often unless you are performing fairly difficult music.

Examples of demisemiquavers (thirty-second notes)

Triplets

As you have already seen with the quaver, a beat can be split into two equal parts.

When a beat is divided into three equal parts, it is notated as a triplet. A small number 3 is written over or under the three notes and many times a curved line or bracket is added. If it is a crotchet (quarter note) beat being divided into three, the three notes in the triplet are written as quavers (eighth notes).

⬛COMPACT⬛disc Exercise 5.8 (Listening)

Listen to the following examples using triplets, performed on the CD.

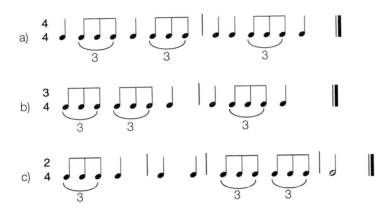

Other less commonly used time signatures

In the following table, you will find some of the less commonly used time signatures.

2 Two beats in each bar 2 Minim (half note) gets one beat	$\frac{2}{2}$ ♩♩ | ♩♩ ‖ 1 2 1 2
4 Four beats in each bar 2 Minim (half note) gets one beat	$\frac{4}{2}$ ♩♩♩♩ | ♩♩♩♩ ‖ 1 2 3 4 1 2 3 4
3 Three beats in each bar 8 Quaver (eighth note) gets one beat	$\frac{3}{8}$ ♫♫♫ | ♫♫♫ ‖ 1 2 3 1 2 3
9 Nine beats in each bar 8 Quaver (eighth note) gets one beat	$\frac{9}{8}$ ♫♫♫ ♫♫♫ ♫♫♫ ‖ 1 2 3 4 5 6 7 8 9
12 Twelve beats in each bar 8 Quaver (eighth note) gets one beat	$\frac{12}{8}$ ♫♫♫ ♫♫♫ ♫♫♫ ♫♫♫ ‖ 1 2 3 4 5 6 7 8 9 10 11 12

Incomplete bars

A piece of music may begin with a bar containing fewer than the required number of beats stated in the time signature. The notes in the incomplete bars are often referred to as pick-up notes. The following example shows music written in $\frac{4}{4}$. There are only three beats in the first bar, but the last bar contains only one beat. Adding the notes of the first and last bars together equals four beats. Examples of popular tunes that start with an incomplete bar include 'Happy Birthday' and 'Oh, When the Saints Go Marching In'.

Examples of music beginning with incomplete bars

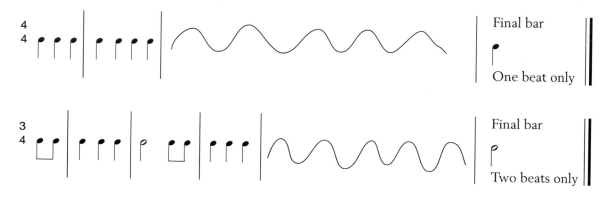

Syncopation

When an expected accent is displaced, rhythms occur where usually weak beats are given strong accents. This is called syncopation and is used in various styles of music, particularly ragtime.

<hr />

GOALS

1 Understand $\frac{3}{4}$ time, including dotted and tied notes.

2 Be able to count quavers (eighth notes).

3 Understand dotted crotchets (quarter notes).

4 Play a rhythm which includes quavers along with the CD.

5 Count and notate semiquavers (sixteenth notes) and triplets.

6 Know the counting of less common time signatures.

7 Understand incomplete bars and syncopation.

Answers

Exercise 5.3

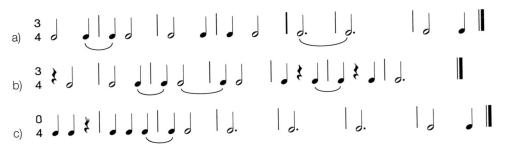

6

Sharps and flats

Sharps and flats are important signs in musical notation. They are used to raise or lower pitches. The structure of key signatures, scales and chords all involve the use of sharps and flats. A clear understanding is therefore needed before moving on to study these topics. Locating sharps and flats on the keyboard provides a good visual starting point.

Sharps and flats on the keyboard

When studying the layout of the keyboard in Unit 2, the black keys were used as 'landmarks' for locating the white keys. Figure 6.1 shows how the black keys get their names from the white.

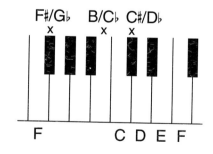

Figure 6.1

If a black key is higher in pitch, i.e. located a semitone (half tone) to the right of the white key, it is called sharp. If, instead, the black key is located to the left of the white, it is called flat. Sharps and flats do not always involve black keys. For example, C♭ is the same as B and F♭ is E. The two different names for the same pitch is called an enharmonic.

Exercise 6.1 (Written)
On the keyboard diagram in Unit 2, locate the following keys up and down the keyboard. Underneath each, write the enharmonic.

A♭   B♭   C♯   E♭   G♯   D♭   F♭   C♭   D♯   B   A♯

G♯ — — — — — — — — — —

Notation for sharps and flats

There are musical signs to show when a pitch is to be raised or lowered.

♯ is sharp   ♭ is flat

When writing a sharp or flat sign beside a note, the sign must be placed before the note and on the same line or space.

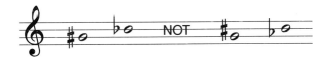

■ Figure 6.2

Exercise 6.2 (Written)

Practise adding sharps and flats to the following notes, then write the letter-names under each. The sign goes before the note on the staff but after the letter-name! This exercise is a good review for reading pitches in both treble and bass clef.

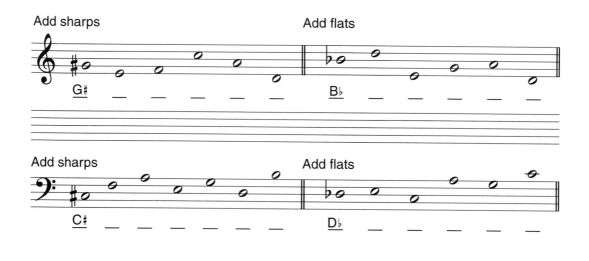

■ Figure 6.3

Accidentals

When a composer wants to alter an individual pitch in a work, a sharp or flat sign is written as needed. These are called accidentals. Once an accidental has been added, it remains 'active' for the rest of that bar. If a note has been made sharp or flat but the composer then wants to return to the original pitch within that same bar, a natural sign, ♮, must be used. A bar line automatically cancels an accidental, so it must be added again if required in the next bar. Note that an accidental only applies to the pitch of the note to which it has been added. If, for example, a sharp has been added to an F on the first space of the treble clef and there is a higher F in the same bar, a sharp must be added to the higher F as well.

Example showing adding accidentals to notes of the same name but of different pitches

■ Figure 6.4

Exercise 6.3 (Listening)

Study the tune 'Accidental Blues'. It is a 12-bar blues, a popular form used in jazz. In blues music, there are many altered pitches called 'blues notes'. These add tension and feeling, helping to set the mood of the music. Listen to 'Accidental Blues' on the CD. The notes are arranged in bass and treble clef and split between left and right hand when played on piano or keyboard. See if you are able to follow the notes.

'Accidental Blues'

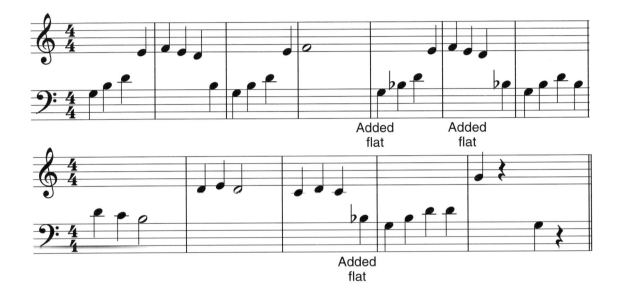

■ Figure 6.5

Double sharps and double flats

There are some occasions when a note already sharpened will be raised yet again. This is called a double sharp, the sign being a cross **✗**. In the example that follows, the double sharp changes the C♯ to C✗. The enharmonic pitch is D. Double sharps function as accidentals and affect all the notes of the same pitch for the rest of the bar unless cancelled. There are different ways of cancelling a double sharp. One way is just to write one sharp in front of the pitch. Another way is to write a natural sign plus one sharp.

Examples of cancelling double sharps

■ Figure 6.6

A double flat, written ♭♭, lowers a pitch which is already flattened. As with double sharps, the sign is added as an accidental and lasts throughout the bar unless cancelled.

Examples of cancelling double flats

■ Figure 6.7

Exercise 6.4 (Written)
Make the following into double sharps or double flats, then write the enharmonic below each one.

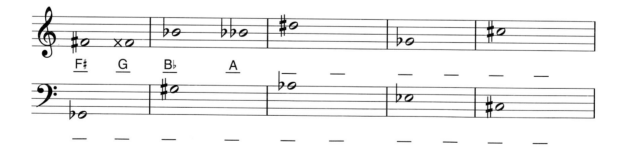

■ Figure 6.8

GOALS

1 Locate sharps and flats on the keyboard.

2 Correctly notate sharps and flats on the staff.

3 Understand the rules for adding and cancelling accidentals.

4 Understand adding and cancelling double sharps and double flats.

Answers

Exercise 6.1

G♯ A♯ D♭ D♯ A♭ C♯

E B E♭ C♭ B♭

Exercise 6.2

Exercise 6.4

Figure 6.9

7

Intervals

An interval is the distance between two pitches and may be large or small. It is important to have a thorough understanding and working knowledge of intervals, as scale and chord construction, which will be studied later in this book, are based on arrangements of intervals. Also, being able quickly to recognize how written intervals sound helps in sight reading and in following musical scores. This unit will help you understand about writing intervals, as well as recognizing their different sounds. It would be helpful to have the keyboard diagram handy while studying intervals.

Semitones and whole tones

The closest distance in pitch between two notes is the semitone or half tone. Examples are C moving up to D♭ or F♯ moving up to G. On the keyboard, a semitone is not necessarily a white key moving to a black. E to F are semitones as are B to C. There are no black keys between E and F or B and C. The interval made of two semitones is called a whole tone or simply tone. C moving up to D is a tone, comprising of C to D♭ (semitone) and the D♭ to D (semitone). Intervals may be built either upwards or downwards from a given note.

Exercise 7.1 (Written)

The following is a series of semibreves (whole notes). Some are in treble clef, others are in bass. For the first group, draw the note which is a semitone higher than the given note, and write the letter-names of both notes. Remember that an interval shows the distance between two notes. A semitone above G, for example, can be written as either G♯ or A♭. However, when identifying intervals, use the notation that shows movement from one note to another, in this case, the A♭.

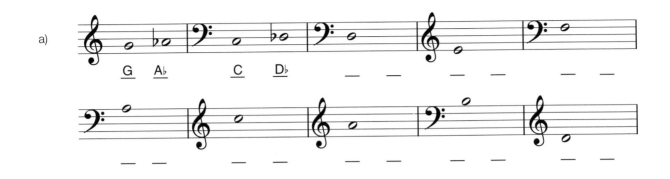

G A♭   C   D♭   __ __   __ __   __ __

■ Figure 7.1

For this group, draw the note which is a semitone lower than the given note. Follow the rest of the instructions as already given.

A G♯   __ __   __ __   __ __   __ __

■ Figure 7.2

For the final group, draw the note a whole tone higher than the given note, then name both notes. Warning: the intervals between E to F and B to C are tricky.

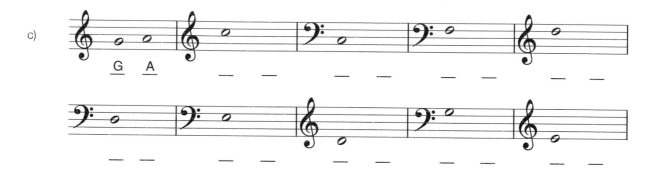

■ Figure 7.3

Other intervals

There are five different types of interval: major, minor, perfect, augmented and diminished. The major and perfect intervals will be explained first. The name of an interval is determined by the number of scale steps involved and relationship to the first note, the keynote. The unison is the term given to the same note as the starting note.

Because intervals involve the space between two notes, two separate parts need to be notated to show this. In the next example, middle C is the keynote. The other intervals are counted from C which is number 1. The intervals of the fourth, fifth and octave are called perfect intervals, abbreviated by P. The second, third, sixth and seventh are major intervals with the abbreviation of M.

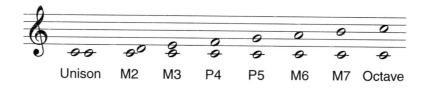

■ Figure 7.4

Each interval contains a certain number of semitones from the keynote. The table that follows shows the number of semitones which make up each interval, counting upwards from the keynote. When constructing an interval, always count the keynote as one. You can find any interval above a given note by counting the semitones upwards from this given note.

Interval	
Major second	2 semitones
Major third	4
Perfect fourth	5
Perfect fifth	7
Major sixth	9
Major seventh	11

Exercise 7.2 (Written)

Counting upwards from the bottom note which acts as the keynote for each, construct the interval above the given note. Some intervals will require the addition of a sharp or flat as shown in the example to make the number of semitones required for the interval correct.

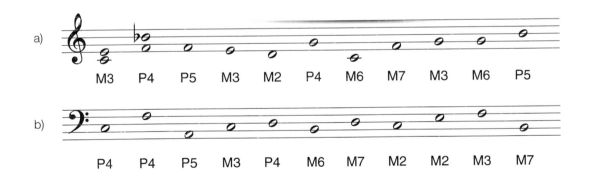

■ Figure 7.5

Exercise 7.3 (Listening and practical)

On the CD, you will hear a demonstration of the sounds of different intervals found within the octave. Helpful information will be given as to how to recognize different intervals. Listen to the intervals played on the CD. Each will be repeated three times. You need to write down the interval you think you heard. This gives practice in recognizing the sounds of various intervals and is especially helpful in sight reading or sight singing.

Minor, diminished and augmented intervals

A major interval becomes minor by lowering the top note one semitone or raising the bottom note that same distance. If it is made another semitone smaller, the interval then becomes diminished.

Examples of minor and diminished intervals

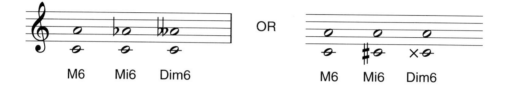

■ Figure 7.6

Perfect intervals become diminished if made a semitone smaller. They do not become minor.

Examples of perfect intervals made diminished

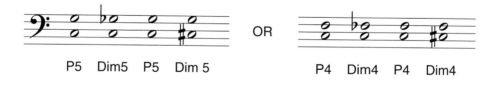

■ Figure 7.7

Major and perfect intervals become augmented intervals if expanded by one semitone. The augmented fourth/diminished fifth is known as the tritone because it contains three whole tones. Until the 20th century, the tritone was considered to be a particularly dissonant and restless interval which needed to be used carefully, having the tension it created properly resolved.

The example that follows shows minor, diminished and augmented intervals using middle C as the keynote. Notice that the augmented fourth and diminished fifth are the same, as are the augmented fifth and minor sixth. These are called enharmonic intervals. Don't worry about diminished and augmented seconds, thirds, sixths and sevenths. These are very rarely used.

Unison   Mi2   Mi3   Dim4   Aug4   Dim5   Aug5   Mi6   Mi7

 Figure 7.8

The following table shows the number of semitones contained in minor, diminished and augmented intervals.

Interval	
Minor second	1 semitone
Minor third	3
Diminished fourth	4
Augmented fourth	6
Diminished fifth	6
Augmented fifth	8
Minor sixth	8
Minor seventh	10

Exercise 7.4 (Written)

The following is a series of major intervals. Change them to minor by adding the necessary accidentals to the upper note.

a)

M3　Mi3　M6　Mi6　M2　Mi2　M7　Mi7　M3　Mi3

■ Figure 7.9

Now change the following perfect intervals to diminished or augmented as indicated.

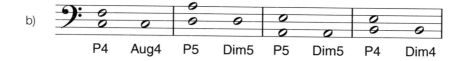

b)

P4　Aug4　P5　Dim5　P5　Dim5　P4　Dim4

■ Figure 7.10

○ISC Exercise 7.5 (Listening and practical)

First listen to examples of minor, augmented and diminished intervals. A series will then be played for you to identify the type of interval. Jot down your answers as you listen.

Inverted intervals

An interval may be inverted by moving the lower note an octave higher or the higher note an octave lower. When inverted, a perfect interval remains perfect, but a major interval becomes minor and a diminished interval becomes augmented. The original number of the interval and the number of its inversion always equals nine. In the following examples, a) shows the lower note moved to the top, while b) shows the higher note moved to the bottom.

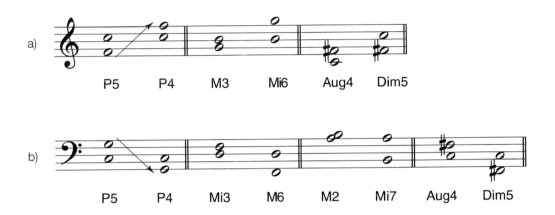

■ Figure 7.11

Compound intervals

Compound intervals are larger than an octave. The interval of a ninth is an octave plus one step. An octave plus two steps is called a tenth. Beyond the interval of a tenth, the octave is not counted. The interval of the eleventh is, therefore, called a fourth. An interval remains the same type even though an octave is added. A major second is also a major ninth.

Examples of compound intervals

M9   M10   Mi10

■ Figure 7.12

GOALS

1 Define the term 'interval'.

2 Know the difference between a semitone and whole tone.

3 Construct intervals above a given keynote.

4 Recognize the sounds of different intervals found within an octave (i.e. second, third, fourth).

5 Be able to write and recognize when played the different types of interval (i.e. major, minor, augmented and diminished).

6 Understand inverted and compound intervals.

Answers

Exercise 7.1

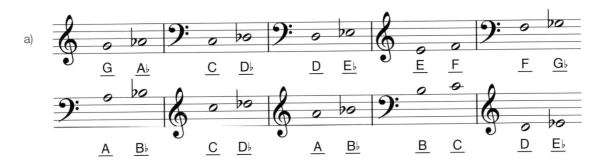

■ Figure 7.13

■ Figure 7.14

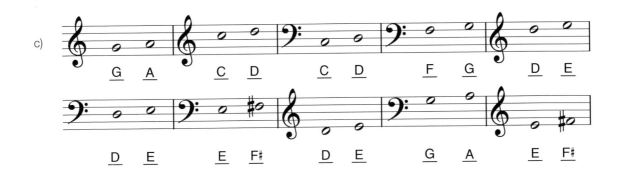

■ Figure 7.15

Exercise 7.2

a)   M3   P4   P5   M3   M2   P4   M6   M7   M3   M6   P5

■ Figure 7.16

b)   P4   P4   P5   M3   P4   M6   M7   M2   M2   M3   M7

■ Figure 7.17

Exercise 7.3

P4   M3   M2   Octave   P5   M3   P4   M6   M7

Exercise 7.4

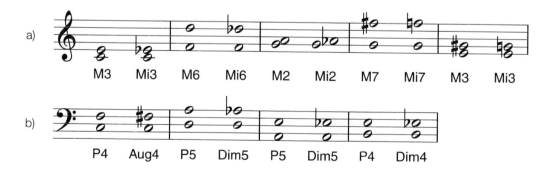

a)   M3   Mi3   M6   Mi6   M2   Mi2   M7   Mi7   M3   Mi3

b)   P4   Aug4   P5   Dim5   P5   Dim5   P4   Dim4

 ■ Figure 7.18

8

More about intervals

I n the previous unit, you learned about the construction of individual intervals and how they
sound when played together. These are harmonic intervals. In this unit you will discover how
intervals are linked together in music to form complete melodies. These are melodic intervals.

COMPACT disc **Exercise 8.1 (Listening and written)**

Look at the following short melody of eight bars, written in treble clef. Listen to it on the CD, following the notes as the tune is
played. After your listening, mark the intervals between the notes with brackets. Some move upwards from the previous note,
others downwards. For further practice, this exercise can be carried out on any piece of music.

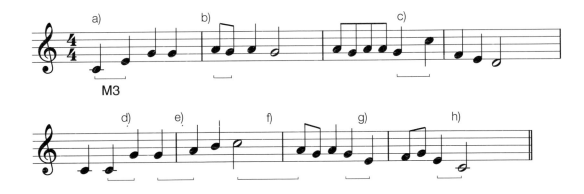

■ Figure 8.1

Sight reading

Sight reading is a skill which needs continuous practice. It involves being able to look at a piece of written music and knowing what it sounds like, even before hearing it performed. There are different ways to approach a tune you want to sight read. The following exercise will take you through some of the steps.

Exercise 8.2 (Practical)
The following tune is a familiar one and you should be able to identify it by studying it in various ways. First, quickly look through the piece, noticing the clef, time signature and any added sharps or flats. Try clapping the rhythm, then analysing the way the notes move. The first three notes in this tune are repeats of C. These are followed by a step moving upwards and two more repeated notes. See if you can sing the first eight bars of the melody. You might use 'la' or the letter-names of the notes. Check the name of the tune at the back of the unit before moving on to the next exercise.

■ Figure 8.2

Transposing

Transposing involves moving all the notes of a piece of music the same distance up or down. It is used to put music into a range which is more comfortable for a player or singer. Transposing a melody up or down an octave is fairly easy because the names of the notes stay the same.

Exercise 8.3 (Written)

Transpose 'Row, Row, Row' up one octave from bass clef to treble clef.

■ Figure 8.3

Now transpose it up the interval of a perfect fourth from your version in treble clef. Check your starting note with the back of the unit before completing the entire transposition.

■ Figure 8.4

Exercise 8.4 (Listening)

Listen to 'Row, Row, Row' played, transposed in different ways.

music theory

COMPACT DISC **Exercise 8.5 (Practical)**

How many times have you wished you could write down a melody you have heard in music notation? This exercise will show you the basics of how to do this by using melodic dictation. There follow skeletons for two short melodies of four bars each. On the CD, each melody will be played five times. There will be a pause after each repetition to give you a chance to write down what you have heard. Try to listen for intervals you recognize in the melody. On each listening, it is best to try to get something written down for every bar, adding more on each repetition.

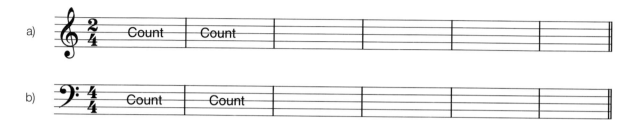

■ Figure 8.5

GOALS

1 Be able to analyse the intervals of a melody line.

2 Know the steps for sight reading music.

3 Understand basic transposition.

4 Write down a simple melody from music dictation.

Answers

Exercise 8.1

a) M3   b) M2   c) P4   d) P5   e) M2   f) Mi3   g) Mi3   h) M3

Exercise 8.2

'Row, Row, Row Your Boat'

Exercise 8.3

Starting note first space F; a perfect fourth above middle C.

Exercise 8.5

■ Figure 8.6

9

Major scales and key signatures

Introduction to different types of scale

A scale is the alphabetical succession of notes beginning on a particular pitch. The word is derived from the Latin, *scala* which means ladder. All music is composed using some form of scale. Many different types of scale have been used in music through the ages, from ancient church modes, folk music of different lands to the innovative 12-tone row devised in the 20th century. Scales sound different from one another because of the way the pitches are arranged. In medieval music, the various scale formations were called modes, each having its own individual arrangement of whole tones and semitones. We will begin the study of scales by listening to some examples on the CD.

◎ CD Exercise 9.1 (Listening)

This exercise is designed to give you a general idea of the sound of different modes. Try to follow the notation as you listen to each example as it is played on the keyboard.

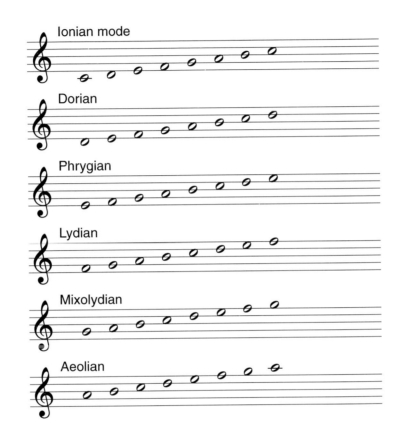

■ Figure 9.1

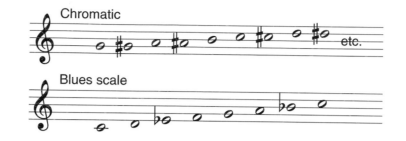

■ Figure 9.2

Major scale construction

For approximately the past 400 years, most music in the Western world has used major or minor scales, the old medieval modes of Ionian and Aeolian. This unit will deal with the major scale, first looking at how it is constructed.

A major scale is a series of semitones and whole tones arranged in a specific order. It is this arrangement that identifies it as major in sound. The notes for a C major scale can be found by playing just the white keys from any C to the C an octave higher. The notes contained in a scale are called degrees, with the starting note, the keynote, defining the tonal centre or key. Music using the scale of C major is referred to as being in the key of C or just 'in C'.

The following example shows the C major scale with degree numbers marked.

■ Figure 9.3

By analysing the intervals between the degrees, we find that there is a mixture of whole tones and semitones.

> C to D is a whole tone
>
> D to E is a whole tone
>
> E to F is a semitone
>
> F to G is a whole tone
>
> G to A is a whole tone
>
> A to B is a whole tone
>
> B to C is a semitone.

The pattern of T T S T T T S has emerged. The abbreviations used are T = tone or whole tone and S = semitone. The eight notes of a major scale may be divided into two sections of four notes each. Each section contains a tetrachord. The semitones occur at the same place in each tetrachord.

■ Figure 9.4

Constructing other major scales

The pattern set by the C major scale must be followed in constructing all major scales. Any note may be used as the starting or keynote, but C is the only major scale not needing any alterations. A major scale starting on any other note will have changes made to the spacing. The intervals are made correct by adding either sharps or flats where needed.

The example that follows shows the construction of a major scale beginning on G. The interval between the E and F is only a semitone. A whole tone is needed at that point. Raising the F to F♯ creates a whole tone. The F♯ also makes a semitone between the F and G as required by the pattern.

G   E   F♯   G

■ Figure 9.5

Exercise 9.2 (Written)

This exercise gives you further practice in constructing major scales. See if you are able to construct major scales beginning and ending on F, A, B♭ and E. Remember to follow the pattern of T T S T T T S. It remains the same for all major scales, even if the starting note begins on a sharp or flat. Since the C major scale is the only major scale having no sharps or flats, some changes will be needed in the other series to make them fit the pattern. Either sharps or flats are used, depending on what needs to be altered.

■ Figure 9.6

Key signatures

The information at the beginning of a work, showing sharps or flats, is called the key signature. The only note altered in the series of notes from G to G was the F. It became F♯, which is the key signature for the key of G major. In this instance, the ♯ is written at the beginning of the piece to indicate that all Fs throughout the work will be sharp, whether pitched high or low. The key signature is repeated at the beginning of every line of music, unlike the time signature which only appears once at the start of a work. Note that the F♯ cannot be written as a G♭. This would make two Gs (G and G♭) in the scale and no F. Each degree of the scale must be present.

Key signature for G major

■ Figure 9.7

Any key signature will use either sharps or flats. They are never mixed. You won't see a signature like this example. If you do, it's wrong!

Notation of key signatures

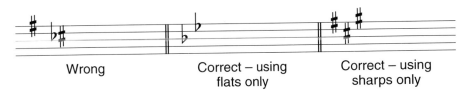

Wrong   Correct – using   Correct – using
                     flats only   sharps only

■ Figure 9.8

Exercise 9.3 (Written)
This exercise shows the difference between adding accidentals and writing key signatures. You may be asked to write a scale and add the alterations (accidentals) to the series of notes. If this is the case, do not write the key signature at the beginning. Using both is wrong. To help in learning the pattern of a major scale, mark all the semitones. Complete the following scales, carefully following the instructions:

a) Write a scale from G to G, ascending. Include the key signature at the beginning.

■ Figure 9.9

b) Write a scale from D to D, ascending. Add accidentals to the degrees of the scale where needed.

■ Figure 9.10

c) Write a scale, descending from E, with the key signature included.

■ Figure 9.11

d) Write a scale, both ascending and descending, starting and ending on E♭, with the key signature included.

■ Figure 9.12

The circle of fifths

It is not necessary to memorize all the key signatures. The circle of fifths is an easy way to find a key signature (see Figure 9.13).

For keys having sharps in the signature, start with C, located at the top. Move clockwise to G which has one sharp. Move on to D. There is an interval of a fifth between, or seven semitones. Each new key is five letter-names higher than the last, but be sure to count the semitones because some keys begin on a sharp or flat. For flat keys, read the circle anti-clockwise.

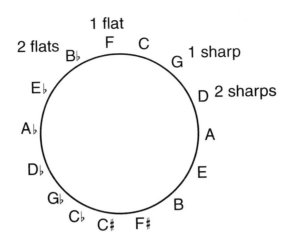

■ Figure 9.13

■ **Exercise 9.4 (Listening)**

Listen to a demonstration of the circle of fifths.

Writing key signatures

Sharps and flats always appear in the same order, the new one added to the ones already there. Study the examples of how sharps and flats are written in both the treble and bass clefs. To learn the correct order, it might be helpful to copy them a few times. A chart containing key signatures is included in the back of the book for future reference.

■ Figure 9.14

Exercise 9.5 (Written)

Using the circle of fifths, write the key signatures for the following major keys:

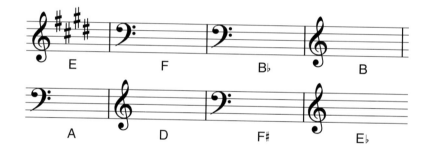

■ Figure 9.15

GOALS

1 Name the medieval modes and their starting note.

2 Understand how to construct a major scale.

3 Define 'key signature'.

4 Be able to find major key signatures by using the circle of fifths.

5 Know how to write sharps and flats as key signatures in the correct order.

Answers

Exercise 9.2

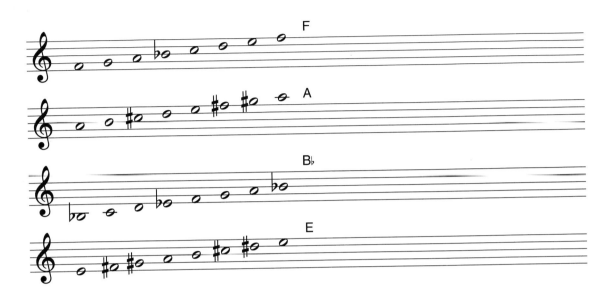

■ Figure 9.16

Exercise 9.3

a) G major scale

■ Figure 9.17

b) D major scale

■ Figure 9.18

c)   E major scale

■ Figure 9.19

d)   E♭ major scale

■ Figure 9.20

Exercise 9.5

E   F   B♭   B

A   D   F#   E♭

■ Figure 9.21

10

Minor scales and key signatures

As well as the major scale, the minor is also commonly used in Western music. This unit explores the minor, starting by comparing its construction to the major. Listening and written work help in understanding the three different forms of minor scales and minor key signatures. Parallel and relative signatures are also covered.

Minor scale construction

Just as C to C produced the pattern for major scales, A to A played on the white notes of the keyboard produces the pattern for the minor. Whereas the major scale has only one form, the minor has three: natural, harmonic and melodic. The A to A scale is the natural form, but the harmonic or melodic forms are more commonly found in music.

Minor scale in
natural form

■ Figure 10.1

For the harmonic minor, the seventh degree is raised one semitone, both ascending and descending. In melodic, the sixth and seventh degrees are raised one semitone when ascending, but cancelled when descending, returning to the natural form. The alterations are added as accidentals where needed throughout the music. The forms of minor scale used may vary within a piece with both the notes of the harmonic and melodic appearing. Because of this, music is said to be in a minor key, not harmonic or melodic minor.

 **Exercise 10.1 (Listening)**

Listen to a demonstration on minor scales. The three different forms follow here.

■ Figure 10.2

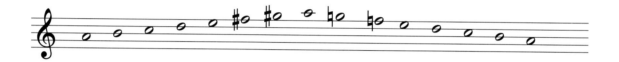

■ Figure 10.3

Natural, harmonic and melodic forms

As with major scales, the minor in its natural form is also constructed using a series of semitones and whole tones. Their arrangement, however, is slightly different from the major scale pattern.

By analysing the intervals in the following example, the minor scale pattern can be found.

■ Figure 10.4

A to B is a whole tone

B to C is a semitone

C to D is a whole tone

D to E is a whole tone

E to F is a semitone

F to G is a whole tone

G to A is a whole tone.

The pattern for constructing a natural minor scale is T S T T S T T.

Exercise 10.2 (Written)

Using the pattern, construct a natural minor scale beginning on E. Add any accidentals needed to alter the intervals.

■ Figure 10.5

Which note would be raised to make the harmonic minor? (Remember, it is the same both ascending and descending.)

Write the melodic minor scale here, both ascending and descending, adding accidentals.

■ Figure 10.6

Before moving on, complete the following questions:

a) Write a harmonic minor scale, ascending and descending, starting on the given note. Use a key signature.

■ Figure 10.7

b) Write a melodic minor scale, ascending and descending, starting on the given note. Use accidentals only.

■ Figure 10.8

Key signatures

Like the major scales, there is also a relationship of a fifth for finding minor key signatures.

Starting at the A which has no sharps or flats, read clockwise to find the signature for keys containing sharps, anti-clockwise for flats.

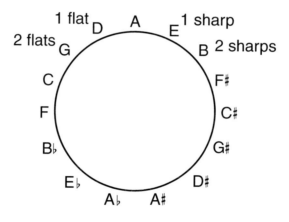

■ Figure 10.9

Exercise 10.3 (Written)

Using the circle of fifths, write the key signature for the following minor keys:

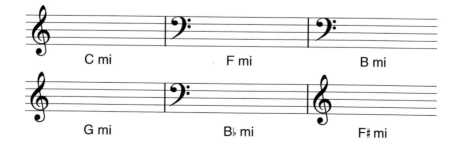

■ Figure 10.10

Parallel and relative minor key signatures

Minor key signatures relate to the major in two different ways, parallel and relative. C major and C minor are parallel. They have the same letter-name but different key signatures. C major has no sharps or flats but C minor has three flats. Relative keys have the same key signature but different letter-names. C major has no sharps or flats and A minor has no sharps or flats. If you know the major key signatures, it is easy to find a parallel minor key signature. For example, to find the parallel minor signature for C major, count up three semitones from C. This brings you to Eb. The key signature for Eb major is three flats, the same as C minor!

Exercise 10.4 (Written)

Write the parallel key signatures for each of the following keys:

 Figure 10.11

The blues scale

The blues scale was introduced to you at the beginning of the unit on major scales. It is a hybrid scale, being a major scale with a lowered third and seventh. These alterations are made to add feeling and emotion to blues music.

Example of major scale with 'blues' alterations

■ Figure 10.12

Exercise 10.5 (Listening)

Finally, to end the two units on scales, I have composed a short tune called 'Fishy Scales'. Within the piece, I have used several types of scales, some of which were introduced to you at the beginning of the unit on major scales. These have been marked on your music. Listen for the differences.

'Fishy Scales'

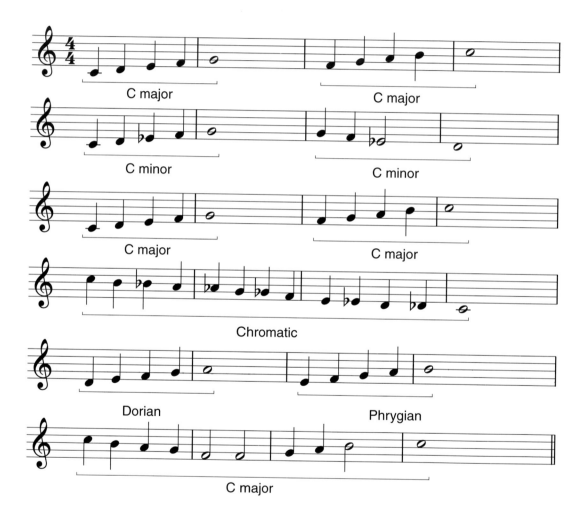

■ Figure 10.13

GOALS

1 Understand the construction of the natural minor scale.

2 Know the names and differences in the three forms of minor scale.

3 Find minor key signatures by using the circle of fifths.

4 Know the difference between parallel and relative minor.

Answers

Exercise 10.2

E – natural minor scale

■ Figure 10.14

D♯ raised for harmonic minor scale

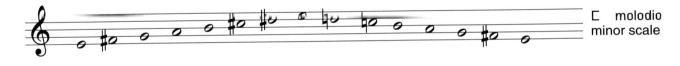

E molodio minor scale

■ Figure 10.15

a)

D – harmonic minor

■ Figure 10.16

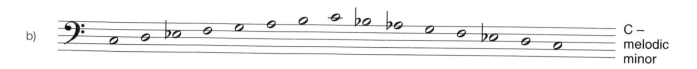

b) C –
melodic
minor

Figure 10.17

Exercise 10.3

C mi = 3 flats

G mi = 2 flats

F minor = 4 flats

B♭ mi = 5 flats

B minor = 2 sharps

F♯ minor = 3 sharps

Exercise 10.4

a)   A minor = no sharps or flats

B minor = 2 sharps

b)   F minor = 4 flats

B♭ minor = 5 flats

C♯ minor = 4 sharps

11

Compound time signatures

In order to participate in music, whether as a listener, player or singer, it is important to understand how to count in various time signatures. A melody is completely unrecognizable if the rhythm is incorrect. So far in this book, you have learned about the time signatures of $\frac{2}{4}$, $\frac{3}{4}$, and $\frac{4}{4}$. These are referred to as simple time signatures. There is another set of signatures for compound time, the most common being $\frac{6}{8}$.

Counting $\frac{6}{8}$

In the time signature of $\frac{6}{8}$, there are six beats in each bar. The difference is that now the quaver (eighth note) gets the beat instead of the crotchet (quarter note). The first beat is strong, followed by two weak beats on 2 and 3. The fourth beat is medium strong, but not as strong as the first beat. Beats 5 and 6 are weak. Quavers (eighth notes) are grouped as follows:

In $\frac{6}{8}$, the two strong beats on 1 and 4 give an underlying feel of counting in two. In fact, if music written in $\frac{6}{8}$ is to be performed at a fast tempo, it is usually conducted in two, not six.

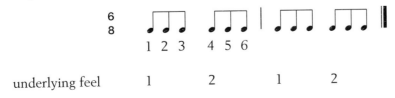

When notating quavers in $\frac{6}{8}$, join them so that the division between the third and fourth beats is clear.

1 2 3 4 5 6   1 2 3 4 5 6

correct   wrong

Exercise 11.1 (Listening)

Music written in $\frac{6}{8}$ time has a lilting feel, like someone skipping. Popular tunes which use $\frac{6}{8}$ include 'I Saw Three Ships', 'For He's a Jolly Good Fellow' and 'Greensleeves'. Hum these tunes to yourself and see if you are able to feel the lilting rhythm. Listen to a demonstration of $\frac{6}{8}$ played on the keyboard. You should be able to hear the six quavers (eighth notes) as well as the two underlying strong beats on the first and fourth counts of each bar.

Exercise 11.2 (Written)

Complete the written exercises using $\frac{6}{8}$ by adding notes, stems or rests as needed.

Add bar-lines to make the following into $\frac{6}{8}$.

Exercise 11.3 (Practical)

Practise clapping these ⁶₈ rhythms. Remember to count two bars before you start clapping.

c) This one is written in two parts. Learn each part, then tap one part with your left hand while your right taps the other!

COMPACT ᴅɪsᴄ Exercise 11.4 (Practical)

For the final exercise using ⁶₈, you will be playing along with the CD. Here is the music for a short piece of music. While the tune is played, you are to clap the rhythm along to the music. Instructions will be given before you start.

■ Figure 11.1

Other compound time signatures

Besides $^6_8$, the time signatures of $^9_8$ and $^{12}_8$ are occasionally found in music.

In $^9_8$ time, there are nine quavers (eighth notes) to each bar, the quaver still receiving one beat. There is an underlying feel of three.

For $^{12}_8$ time, there are 12 quavers (eighth notes) to each bar, the quaver getting one beat. There is an underlying feeling of four.

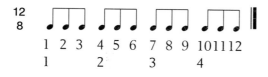

disc Exercise 11.5 (Listening)

Listen to a demonstration of $^9_8$ and $^{12}_8$ time.

Comparing simple and compound time

The following table shows a comparison between simple and compound time signatures.

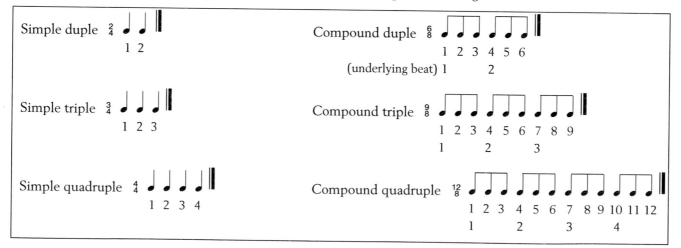

$\frac{5}{8}$ and $\frac{7}{8}$

In the time signatures of $\frac{5}{8}$ and $\frac{7}{8}$, the accents can be arranged in different ways as shown here:

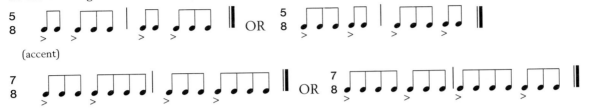

(accent)

Exercise 11.6 (Practical)

Practice clapping the previous example, noticing the difference in feel when the accent is changed.

Exercise 11.7 (Practical – rhythm dictation)

The skeletons for three rhythms follow. Each will be played five times, with gaps left in between each playing for you to write down what you heard. Notice the time signature before starting each one.

a) $\frac{6}{8}$

b) $\frac{9}{8}$

c) $\frac{5}{8}$

GOALS

1 Know the meaning of the time signature of $\frac{6}{8}$.

2 Be able to write and perform $\frac{6}{8}$ rhythms correctly.

3 Understand the compound time signatures of $\frac{9}{8}$ and $\frac{12}{8}$ and their underlying feel.

4 Be able to compare simple and compound time signatures.

5 Clap $\frac{5}{8}$ and $\frac{7}{8}$ time with varying accents.

6 Complete rhythm dictation of four bars, using different time signatures.

Answers

Exercise 11.2

Bar-lines

Exercise 11.7

12

Introducing chords

You have already learned how different rhythms and pitches are combined to form melodies. Music having only a single melody line with no accompaniment is called monophonic. This style was used by the ancient Greeks and in Gregorian chant, the music of the Roman Catholic church named after Pope Gregory I, dating from around 600 AD. Other examples of monophonic music include oriental music and folk songs. When accompaniment is added to a melody line, the music becomes fuller and richer. Using chords is one way of enhancing a melody.

Three or more notes sounded together make a chord. Two notes sounded together is considered an interval, not a chord. There is no limit to the number of notes in a chord and some instruments such as the piano or guitar can play more than one single pitch at one time. Chords are also formed when two or more musicians or singers sound different notes which blend together. The notes of one chord can also be spread throughout the many instruments of an entire symphony.

Major and minor triads

The simplest type of chord is the triad, consisting of three notes. (Think of a tricycle with three wheels or a triangle with three sides.) When the triad is in root position, the root is the lowest note in the chord, with the third and fifth written above it, arranged in intervals of a third. The two basic types of triads are major and minor. In the major, the interval between the root and third is a major third or four semitones. The interval between the third and fifth is a minor third or three semitones. In a minor triad, the intervals are reversed. The interval between the root and third is a minor third and the major third is now found between the third and fifth. Although there is only a slight difference in the construction between major and minor triads, their sounds are quite unique. In simple terms, a major triad sounds bright and cheerful while the minor is sad and mysterious (see Figure 12.1).

Examples of major and minor triads with intervals marked

C   D   G   C mi   D mi G mi

■ Figure 12.1

COMPACT disc Exercise 12.1 (Listening)

Study the examples of major and minor triads that follow. Notice how accidentals have been added to form the correct intervals. The triads are written in root position with the lowest note actually being the root note. Listen to the demonstration of the triads as they are played.

Examples of
major triads

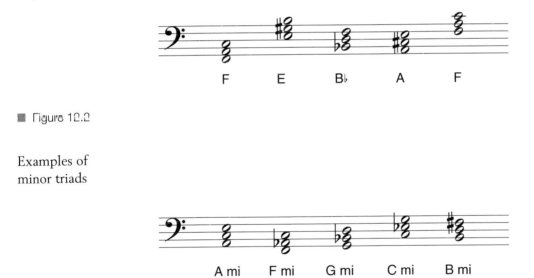

F   E   B♭   A   F

■ Figure 12.2

Examples of
minor triads

A mi   F mi   G mi   C mi   B mi

■ Figure 12.3

Major and minor triads
on the keyboard

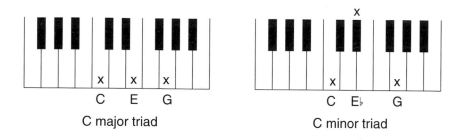

C major triad   C minor triad

■ Figure 12.4

Exercise 12.2 (Written)
Write either a major or minor triad as indicated in root position, adding accidentals where needed.

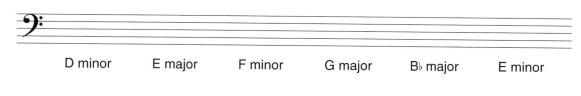

D minor   E major   F minor   G major   B♭ major   E minor

■ Figure 12.5

Inversions

Triads are often used in an arrangement where the root note of the chord is not the lowest. The notes used in the triad stay the same, but they are arranged in a different order. These are called inversions of a triad.

The first example a) shows C and G major triads written in three different positions or inversions. In each, the bottom note has been moved to the top and is an octave higher. The second example b) shows a C major chord moving to a G major chord. The movement is made much easier by using the first inversion of the G chord. Example c) shows a minor triad with inversions.

a) C triad   G triad

■ Figure 12.6

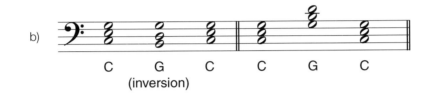

b) C   G   C   C   G   C
       (inversion)

■ Figure 12.7

c) F minor

■ Figure 12.8

Exercise 12.3 (Written)

Practise writing inversions for the following triads:

■ Figure 12.9

Augmented and diminished triads

Major and minor triads can be altered to become augmented and diminished. Augmenting a chord creates more space between the intervals of the third and fifth in root position. Augmented triads are easily made by starting with a major triad in root position and raising the fifth one semitone. A diminished triad is easily made from a minor triad in root position and lowering the fifth one semitone. This reduces the space between the third and fifth (see Figure 12.10).

Examples of augmented and diminished triads

■ Figure 12.10

Keyboard examples showing augmented and diminished triads

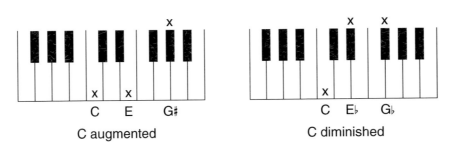

C augmented   C diminished

■ Figure 12.11

COMPACT disc Exercise 12.4 (Listening)

Listen to the demonstration about constructing augmented and diminished triads. Their sound will be compared to that of major and minor triads.

Exercise 12.5 (Written)

Change the following major triads to augmented by adding the necessary accidentals:

a)

Make diminished triads out of the following minor triads, adding accidentals where needed:

b)

■ Figure 12.12

Chord symbols

In popular music especially, a type of abbreviation is used to indicate the accompaniment chords. For a major chord, just the letter-name appears. For minor, a small m is placed after the letter-name. Aug. or + denote augmented chords and dim. or ○ are used for diminished. Chord symbols are most commonly written above the melody line and are used in guitar and keyboard music. The complete chord is not written out in full. The musician is expected to know how to construct the given chords from the symbols.

Example of chord symbols written above the staff and located at the beginning of each bar

■ Figure 12.13

Exercise 12.6 (Practical)

Identify the type of chord you hear as either major, minor, augmented or diminished. Write your answers in the blank spaces, using chord symbols.

_____   _____   _____   _____   _____   _____   _____

_____   _____   _____   _____   _____   _____

Added note chords

The seventh chord

Extra notes are often added to the basic triad to give interest and colour. The seventh above the root note is the most common and the interval of a minor seventh is mostly used. For chord symbols, a small 7 is added following the letter-name. Any type of triad, whether major, minor, augmented or diminished, can have an added seventh.

Examples of seventh chords written in root position with added chord symbols

■ Figure 12.14

The seventh chord has three inversions instead of two because there are now four notes in the chord, not three.

Inversions of the seventh chord

D7

■ Figure 12.15

The idea of adding notes to a triad may be carried further to form chords containing a ninth, eleventh and thirteenth above the root note. Although these more elaborate chords add interest, they also create a weaker key feeling because of the added notes which do not belong to the basic triad. Chords with added notes are found in jazz and also in impressionistic music by composers of the romantic era (1820–1900) such as Debussy.

Examples of added note chords

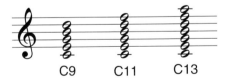

C9   C11   C13

■ Figure 12.16

Exercise 12.7 (Listening)

Listen to a demonstration of different chords with added notes.

Notation of chords

When writing chords out in full on one staff, the stem joins all the notes together. Addition of the stem follows the rule of going upward if the majority of the note heads are below the third line or downwards if the note heads are above the third line. Chords written this way are seen in music for piano. If separate parts are written on the same staff, the stems are written in different directions to separate each part clearly. This is common in vocal music.

Figure 12.17

GOALS

1 Define 'triad'.

2 Know how to construct major and minor triads in root position.

3 Be able to write the inversions of a triad.

4 Construct augmented and diminished triads.

5 Recognize the difference in sound between major, minor, augmented and diminished triads.

6 Construct seventh, ninth, eleventh and thirteenth chords.

7 Understand the correct notation for writing chords.

Answers

Exercise 12.2

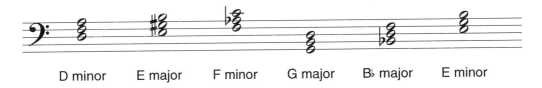

D minor   E major   F minor   G major   B♭ major   E minor

■ Figure 12.18

Exercise 12.3

E minor

A major

F major

■ Figure 12.19

Exercise 12.5

Aug.   Dim.

■ Figure 12.20

Exercise 12.6

Major, minor, major, major, aug., dim., major, minor, aug., dim., minor, aug., aug., major.

13

Harmony

In the previous unit, you learned about the structure of individual chords. This unit goes further in explaining the relationships between chords within a scale and also covers some of the basics of counterpoint. In music where the melody is supported by chords, the texture is referred to as harmonic, harmony being the study of chords. Another approach to adding texture is by writing melodies against each other. This is called counterpoint and the music is referred to as polyphonic.

Chord names and functions

Triads can be built on each degree of a scale. The mode, either major or minor, does not matter. Roman numerals are used to identify each chord. They also have names which show their function and placement within the scale.

Example of triads
built on the scale of C

■ Figure 13.1

I	*Tonic* – the keynote. The name of the scale is based on this.
II	*Super tonic* – the note directly above the tonic.
III	*Mediant* – located halfway between the tonic and dominant.
IV	*Subdominant* – has the same relationship to the upper tonic note as the dominant has from the starting tonic, that of a fifth.
V	*Dominant* – next in importance to the tonic in establishing key feeling.
VI	*Submediant* – midway between the tonic and subdominant.
VII	*Leading tone* – a chord with the strong feeling of leading to the tonic.

The most important chords in establishing the key feeling in any scale are the primary triads of I, IV and V. The other triads are referred to as secondary and function as substitutes for the primary triads to add interest and colour to music.

ⓓⓘⓢⓒ Exercise 13.1 (Listening)

Listen to the demonstration of each of the triads of a scale played on the CD.

Cadences

Cadences are found at the end of a musical phrase and provide a pause in the music. The progression of chords leading to the cadence define the strength of the pause, as described in the following. The examples are written for four separate parts called voices. This is chorale style and will be explained in more detail later in this unit.

1   The cadence using V moving to I is called an authentic cadence and has a final feeling about it. Usually a IV chord precedes the V chord, making the chord progression of IV, V, I. The authentic cadence is called perfect if the tonic note is placed in the top and bottom voices.

Example of an authentic cadence in D major

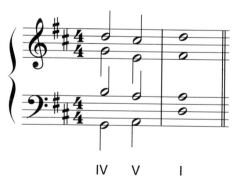

■ Figure 13.2

2   The plagel cadence is a chord progression of IV to I. It is also known as the 'Amen' cadence.

Example of a plagel cadence in C major

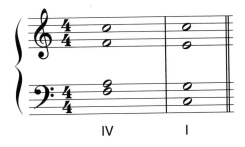

IV   I

■ Figure 13.3

3   A deceptive cadence occurs when the expected tonic chord is replaced by another chord, sometimes the VI. It creates an element of surprise because the expected ending did not happen.

Example of a deceptive cadence in F major

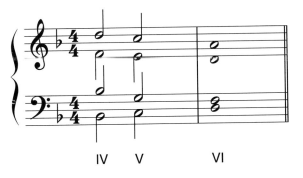

IV   V   VI

■ Figure 13.4

4   The half cadence is a chord progression of I to V.

Example of a half cadence in G major

I   V

■ Figure 13.5

Exercise 13.2 (Listening and practical)

Listen to the musical examples as the cadences are played on the CD. A series of cadences will then be played for you to identify. Jot down your answers as you listen.

Chorale style

Writing chords in four voice parts, also called the chorale style, is the beginning point for the study of harmony. When writing a triad for four voices, one note of the chord will need to be used twice. Where possible, the root is the best note to double. Before actually starting to write in chorale style, it is helpful first to practise writing chords with just the root note in the bass and the rest of the chord in root position in the treble clef.

Exercise 13.3 (Written)

Write the following chords with the root note in the bass and the rest of the chord in treble clef, root position. An example has been done for you.

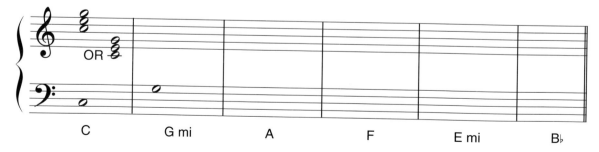

■ Figure 13.6

Four voices split equally

The four voices used in basic chorale style are based on the human voices of soprano, alto, tenor and bass. Their ranges are shown in the example.

Ranges of the human voice

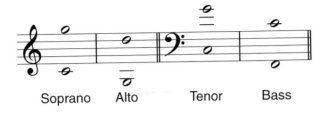

Soprano   Alto   Tenor   Bass

■ Figure 13.7

The rule of doubling the root note still applies, but the voices are now split equally between the treble and bass clefs, the soprano and alto in the treble and tenor and bass voices in the bass clef. The following example shows a chord progression of I, IV, V, I in the key of G major. Although inversions may be used, the example uses all the chords in root position. When inversions are used, small numbers called figured bass are written below the Roman numerals to identify the inversions. Notice the directions of the stems in chorale style. The soprano and tenor stems go up while the alto and bass go down. This is done to separate the parts clearly and make reading easier. Basic rules of four-part writing state that there should not be more than an octave between each voice part except for the lowest two voices. Notes common to two consecutive chords should be held over and the leading tone must rise to the tonic note to resolve the tension created.

Example of four-part writing

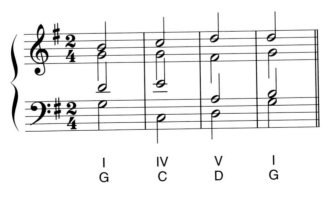

I   IV   V   I
G   C   D   G

■ Figure 13.8

Listen to a demonstration of the last example.

Figured bass

Understanding figured bass is an involved process, but the example that follows gives a very general idea of how these numbers are used. As previously mentioned, small numbers called figured bass define the inversions of chords used. Look at the example of a C major chord in first inversion. Assuming that the C chord is the I chord in the key, the figured bass would be written I_3^6. This means that there is a note the interval of a sixth written somewhere above the bass note. This would be the note C. The G is the note an interval of a third above the bottom note, E. (Note that the G octave is not counted or the interval would be compound, that of a tenth.)

Example of figured bass

$$I \quad {6 \atop 3}$$

■ Figure 13.9

Counterpoint

Counterpoint is a way of adding texture to music by writing melodies against other melodies. Each part is called a voice. Many people feel that counterpoint is difficult to understand with its various melodic lines competing against one another. However, imitation is important to counterpoint and anyone who has ever participated in singing a simple tune as a round with the melody entering at several points has helped create counterpoint!

Instead of a long flowing melody, short, brief melodic figures called motifs are used in counterpoint. One form commonly used in writing counterpoint is the fugue. It is usually in two or three voices and has a subject that enters in various ways throughout the voices to form an interesting and intricate texture.

Example of simple counterpoint written for two voices

 Figure 13.10

Modulation

When you studied scales, the emphasis was on establishing a feeling of being in a certain key or tonal centre. This is very important if a piece of music is going to hold together. In spite of this, a composition of any length will become uninteresting if it continually uses just the harmonies available in one key centre. A change of key centre or mode provides variety and a feeling that the piece has moved away from its beginning point. Changing the key centre during a composition is called modulation. It usually occurs at the end of a phrase or section of a larger work, but should only be used after the initial key centre has been firmly established. If modulation occurs too soon, i.e. before the original key is established, the listener may experience some confusion as to key feeling.

There are several ways to change keys within a piece and this depends somewhat on the style of the music. Some modulations are quite abrupt and make the change very noticeable, yet others are much more subtle. Because the many different methods used to change key are beyond the scope of this book, only the most common will be introduced.

Pivot chord

A frequently used modulation is called 'pivot chord'. The transition involves using a chord both common and closely related to both the original key and the new key.

Exercise 13.5 (Listening)

Study the 'jig' that follows. You will see that it is in two sections, each one repeated. The piece begins in the key of F but moves away from it, the first section ending in C. This is confirmed by the B♭ being cancelled by the natural sign, temporarily establishing the key of C major. The second section begins in C major and works its way back to end in F major. The relationship between the keys of F major and C is a fifth. Now listen to 'Jig' played on the CD, noting the change in key in the first section.

'Jig'

■ Figure 13.11

Exercise 13.6 (Listening)

Another way to modulate is the change between relative major and minor keys. Listen to the next example which changes between the relative keys of A minor and C major.

■ Figure 13.12

Exercise 13.7 (Listening)

Use of a chromatic move is much more abrupt than changing to a related key. The example that follows shows a chromatic change by moving from C major to C♯ major. The music is transposed up one semitone. This type of modulation is often used in popular songs at the beginning of a verse to show a movement on in time. Listen to the example on the CD.

■ Figure 13.13

GOALS

1 Know the names and functions of the chords built on each degree of a scale.

2 Understand and recognize cadences.

3 Know the basics of writing chords in four-part chorale style.

4 Define 'counterpoint'.

5 Understand the basic kinds of modulation.

Answers

Exercise 13.2

Plagel, half, deceptive, authentic, half, authentic, plagel.

Exercise 13.3

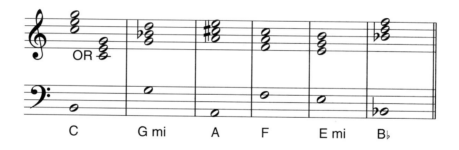

C   G mi   A   F   E mi   B♭

■ Figure 13.14

14

Adding accompaniment to a melody

Especially in popular and folk music, you may come across a written melody having no written accompaniment or chord symbols indicated. A complete study of adding chords and chord progressions is lengthy and beyond the scope of this book. However, this unit attempts to give an introduction to the basic steps involved in adding a simple chord accompaniment to a given melody by using chord symbols.

Finding the most suitable chords

'Folk Tune'

■ Figure 14.1

'Folk Tune' is an easy melody written in the key of C. It needs some chord symbols added as accompaniment. The best way to start is by first writing out a C major scale in treble clef, then building a triad above each scale degree, and marking each chord as major or minor. (Note that the VII chord is diminished and should not be used in this exercise.) It is also helpful to make a chart showing the note names found in each of the triads in the key of C. Remember that the three most important chords in any key are I, IV and V.

Triads in the key of C

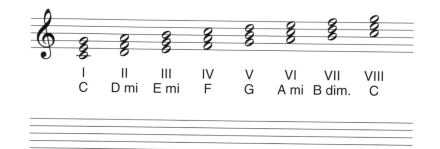

I   II   III   IV   V   VI   VII   VIII
C   D mi   E mi   F   G   A mi   B dim.   C

■ Figure 14.2

Note names found in each triad			
I (C) = C E G	II (D) = D F A	III (E) = E G B	IV (F) = F A C
V (G) = G B D	VI (A) A C E	VII (B) B D F	

When adding chords for accompaniment, keep the process as simple as possible, only changing chords when necessary, usually once or twice per bar. Most simple music begins and ends with the tonic or keynote chord, C in this case. Let's work out an accompaniment for 'Folk Tune'.

The first bar contains two pitches, C and G. Because the tune is in the key of C and both C and G are present in a C major triad, adding a C major chord would be the logical choice for that entire bar. I have written the chord symbol for C above the melody line at the beginning of bar one. The second bar uses only one pitch, F. Because the F major chord is the IV chord, an important chord in the key of C, I have decided to use it, not the D or B chords which are secondary in importance. The third bar is more complicated; now you *are* spoiled for choice! The second note, E, is on a weak beat and serves as a link between the F and D in the melody, but does not affect the choice of chord. Study the chart of note names in each triad: the choices available are either the Dmi or F triad. F has already been used throughout the previous bar, so a change would be welcome. The final two notes of the third bar, D and G, would suggest a G major chord. I would use two chords in that bar, the D minor for the first two beats followed by the G major. The fourth bar is the end of the phrase and needs a cadence. I have again used two chords in that bar, C major and G major, making a half cadence of I to V. The beginning of the next phrase has notes in the melody that outline a C major triad – C, E, G, so C is the obvious choice. In the sixth bar, the important notes are the F and A and suggest either the F chord or the D minor. I think the F chord would be best, followed by the D minor and G in the next bar. This follows the same scheme as in the first phrase.

The second example of 'Folk Tune' shows the most logical chord symbols written above the melody line. The chords in brackets are some of the alternatives.

Exercise 14.1 (Listening)

Turn on the CD and listen to 'Folk Tune' with different chords added as accompaniments. Decide for yourself which ones sound best!

The tune is in the key of C major, so beginning and ending on any chord other than C will not establish the key feeling. Also, bar four is a half cadence, so using the chord of G best defines this.

'Folk Tune'

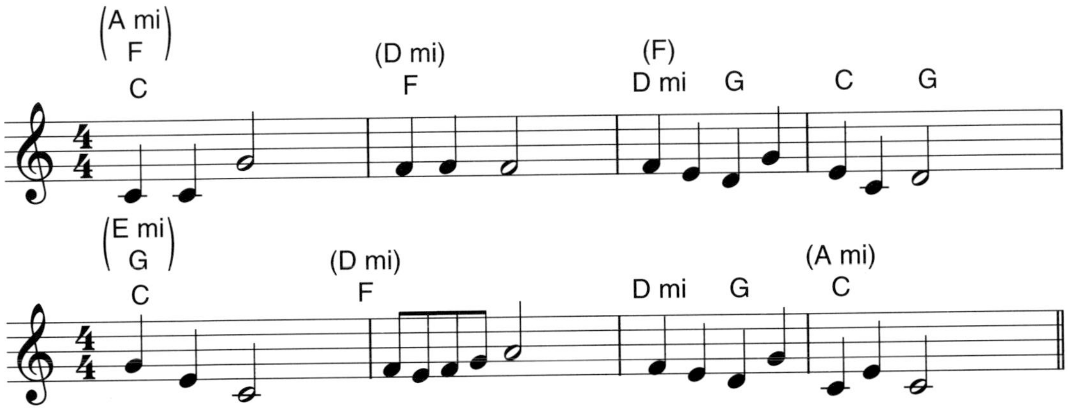

![Folk Tune musical score with chord symbols]

■ Figure 14.3

Exercise 14.2 (Written)

The melody of a well-known tune is written in this exercise in the key of D major. Following the same process as earlier for 'Folk Tune', decide on a simple accompaniment and write the chord symbols above the melody line. Be sure to make a chart showing the names of the notes present in each chord.

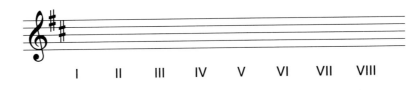

I   II   III   IV   V   VI   VII   VIII

■ Figure 14.4

'The Fox'

■ Figure 14.5

Transposing melody and accompaniment

A lot of music is written in a key which is difficult to sing or play. If this is the case, you will need to transpose both the melody and accompaniment up or down to a more comfortable key. This process is similar to transposing an octave, which you have previously done. It might be helpful to have a diagram of the keyboard available for reference.

Let's look again at 'Folk Tune' written in the key of C. You have decided that it is too low and want to transpose it up to G major. The note G is the interval of a perfect fifth, seven semitones above C. The first step is to transpose all the notes in the melody line up a perfect fifth. The rhythm stays the same, but remember to add the key signature of the new key. Finally, transpose the chord symbols up the interval of a perfect fifth. The example that follows shows 'Folk Tune' transposed to the key of G.

'Folk Tune'

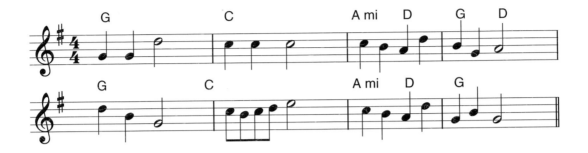

 Figure 14.6

 Exercise 14.3 (Written and listening)

Transpose the melody of 'The Fox' down one whole tone from D major to the key of C, then add the appropriate chord symbols. After you have finished, turn on the CD and listen to 'The Fox' played in both its original key and new key.

'The Fox'

Figure 14.7

Writing an accompaniment

In the previous exercises, the accompaniments were notated as chord symbols, a common method suitable for guitar. The performer usually improvises a suitable accompaniment, using the chord symbols as a guide. Chords functioning as accompaniment may also be written in full music notation. The new example shows 'Folk Tune' (in C) with the accompaniment written in block chords, all in root position. This is a common way to add simple accompaniment to piano or keyboard music. The melody is in the treble clef and played with the right hand. The chords are written in the bass clef and played with the left hand.

Part of 'Folk Tune' with block chords

■ Figure 14.8

Exercise 14.4 (Written)

The first part of the melody for 'The Fox' is written here in the treble clef. Add block chords in root position in the bass clef.

'The Fox'

■ Figure 14.9

COMPACT disc Exercise 14.5 (Listening)

Listen to 'Folk Tune' and 'The Fox' played with block chord accompaniment.

Inversions of chords are often used to make the movements between chords easier. Study the first part of 'Folk Tune' with inversions used in the accompaniment. Notice how much easier it is to move between chords.

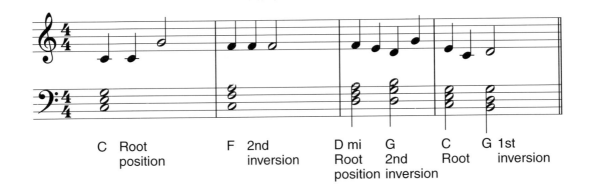

C   Root   F   2nd   D mi   G   C   G 1st
    position   inversion   Root   2nd   Root   inversion
                                      position inversion

■ Figure 14.10

COMPACT disc Exercise 14.6 (Listening)

Besides block chords, there are different ways in which chords can be arranged into interesting patterns. Listen to a demonstration of four examples of accompaniments played on the piano.

GOALS

1 Be able to add basic chords to a simple melody line by using chord symbols.

2 Know how to convert chord symbols into block chords.

3 Transpose melodies and chords to other keys.

15

Musical form

You have seen throughout the book how different elements are combined to make music. However, rhythm, pitch and melody need to be further organized by a basic plan called musical form. The form of a composition functions like a road map. This unit explores some of the basic points about musical forms.

Repetition

Using repetition is one way to help hold a work together. There are special signs used to show when sections of a composition are to be performed more than once. The use of signs saves space and time by removing the need for the music to be written out again.

The repeat sign

One of the most common signs used is called the repeat sign and is written as double lines with two dots placed to the left. When reaching a repeat sign, look for a similar sign with dots on the right and repeat the music contained between the two signs. If there is no matching sign, then return to the beginning of the piece and repeat from there. Once the repeated section has been performed, continue on with the new music after the repeat sign.

COMPACT DISC **Exercise 15.1 (Listening)**

Follow the musical example as it is played, observing the repeats.

a)

b)

■ Figure 15.1

First and second time bars

This type of repeat is similar to the repeat sign. The difference is that on the first performance, a bar marked with a bracket and the number 1 called the first time bar is used. After the second performance, the first time bar is replaced by a different bar called the second time bar. It is marked with a bracket and number 2. Skip over the first time bar and replace it with the second time bar. Do not play the first time bar as well or you will have too many bars in your piece!

Example showing first and second time bars

■ Figure 15.2

Repeated bars

Sometimes, just one bar or even part of a bar is to be repeated several times. A stroke is used to represent each time the bar or section of the bar is to be repeated. To indicate several bars of silence, a long rest sign with the number of bars is used. This is commonly found in music for ensembles.

Examples of repeated bars

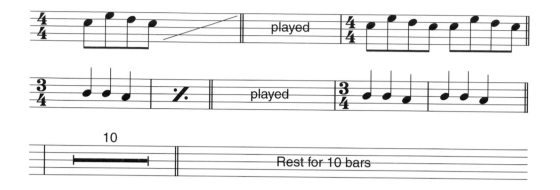

Figure 15.3

DC al fine

The appearance of the words **DC al fine** instructs the performer to return to the beginning of the work and play until reaching the word '**fine**' (finish). The da capo aria is a song form used extensively in opera and provides an opportunity for a soloist to show off his or her vocal capabilities. On the repeat performance, the original material is decorated and embellished, adding to the emotional impact of the aria.

The abbreviation DS means **dal segno**. Instead of returning to the beginning of a work, the performer repeats from where the sign appears.

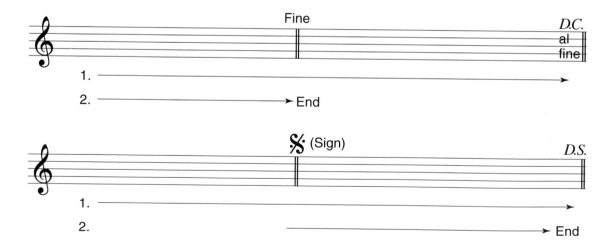

Figure 15.4

Introduction and coda

Many musical works, whether short songs or larger compositions, have an introduction at the beginning. It may range from a few bars to an entire opening section. A coda is found at the end of a work and contains extra bars to give the work a finished feeling. In larger works, the coda may serve as a deception, leading on again when the listener expected the music to end.

Form represented by letters

The plan or design of different music is often diagrammed by using letter-names. Some of the most common forms represented by letters are described in the following sections. These can be found both in individual pieces such as songs or can be part of a much larger work.

Strophic – A A A A A

Music is strophic if all the verses or stanzas are set to the same music. This form is used extensively in hymns and folk tunes. The 'A' represents the use of the same music repeated for every verse although the words change. Sometimes a refrain is used in a strophic song. In this form, there is still a series of verses using the same music. A refrain is a line of lyrics repeated at the end of each verse. The last line of each verse, therefore, uses the same words although the words in the rest of each verse change. An example of a song using a refrain is 'Blowin' in the Wind'.

Theme and variations – A' A'' A''' A''''

In a work of theme and variations, the original melody, the theme, is first presented, usually in a simple style. It is then repeated, but varied in a different way. A 'prime sign' is added for each different variation of the theme.

Binary (two-part) form – A B

A piece written in binary form contains two different sections of music. A common example would be a song having an alternating verse and chorus. This is a form popular for songs because it provides forward movement of the story through each verse alternating with repetition of an important thought restated in the chorus. The music for the verse and chorus are different, the verse being 'A' and the chorus 'B'. The words of each verse change, but the words for the chorus stay the same or nearly the same each time it is repeated.

Ternary (three-part) form – A B A

This is music consisting of three sections. The first and third are the same, with the middle section contrasting.

Rondo – A B A C A D A E

The main characteristic of a rondo is the repetition of the original material, labelled as 'A', alternating with new material. Following each repeat of 'A', new and unrelated music is introduced. It is the constant return of the original music that holds a rondo together.

Sonata or first movement form

This form is frequently used for individual sections or pieces (movements) of a large work. It has three sections, each having a special function. The exposition, beginning in the tonic key, presents the main musical material of the movement. The development section modulates through various keys and builds on the material from the exposition. Finally, the recapitulation more or less repeats the exposition, bringing the work to an ending, back in the tonic key:

Intro (optional)	Exposition	Development section	Recapitulation	Coda (optional)

Composite forms

These are large works having more than one movement, the symphony being an example. It contains the following four movements:

1 Fast, usually in sonata form.

2 Slow, occasionally using theme and variation form.

3 Minuet or other dance.

4 Fast, using rondo or sonata form.

Other composite forms include the concerto – a work for solo instrument and orchestra; sonata – for a solo instrument such as piano; suite – a group of pieces sometimes related by being in the same key.

Words and music

Most of this book has dealt with the various aspects of music on its own, although through the ages, a lot of music has been combined with words. This includes sacred, secular, serious and light. In ancient Greece, music was treated as secondary and largely used to enhance the performance of the dramas. Only a few fragments of Greek music survive. These are three hymns and a drinking song!

After about 1600, opera began to develop and there was renewed controversy as to whether the words or the music were the more important element. Personally, I doubt the question can really be answered and this book is not the place for such a debate. The rest of this unit will briefly explore how words combined with the form of a musical work help in telling stories through songs.

What is a song?

A song is actually a story written in rhyme. The words (lyrics) are set to a single line of melody. Accompaniment is also added to enhance the meaning of the words. The story told by the song can be fact or fiction, but must have a beginning, middle and end. It also must make a point! Just as in any story, there is a main character and maybe some minor ones, too.

Exercise 15.2 (Practical)

Study the lyrics and form of the song 'Love Triangle'. This title suggests a situation that is perhaps common to many. A triangle is also a geometric shape and the chorus uses other shapes to help show the feelings of the singer. Try to imagine how you would feel if you were trapped in a corner of a triangle. You would probably be bent and feel small, unable to stand proud and tall. Think also how you would feel if you loved and trusted someone, then suddenly realized that person had lied about nearly everything. Your mind would probably be going round in circles. Although the singer feels hurt and confused, she is determined to find the strength to get free. She is 'boxed in' but fighting . . . like in a boxing ring. The form of the song is outlined in the lyrics.

'Love Triangle'

Verse 1

A I thought you really loved me, thought that you'd be true.
Couldn't believe I'd found a love wonderful as you.
I thought about you all the time, and how our future'd be,
but I guess I never stopped to think that you would lie to me.

Chorus 1

B I'm trapped in the corner of a love triangle, all because of you.
My head's spinning 'round in circles, don't know what to do.
I'm feeling all boxed in but fighting to get free.
I'm trapped in the corner of a love triangle 'cause you lied to me.

Verse 2

A I knew that you were busy, believed you worked late,
Knew you needed someone patient, someone who would wait.
I believed your every word, you were my whole life,
but I found it hard believing that you have a wife! Now I'm

Chorus 2

B Trapped in the corner of a love triangle, all because of you.
My head's spinning 'round in circles, don't know what to do.
I'm feeling all boxed in but fighting to get free.
I'm trapped in the corner of a love triangle, you and her and me.

Bridge

C Shame . . . shame on you . . . you can't have your cake and eat it too.
Shame . . . shame on you . . . can only serve one love, not two.

B Final chorus – as Chorus 1

GOALS

1 Understand repeat signs.

2 Know how to represent the form of a musical work by using letters.

3 Understand the importance of words and musical form in creating songs.

16

Tone colour and interpretation

ave you ever wondered why the same piece of music performed by two different singers sounds so different even though the song is arranged in exactly the same way? And why does a pitch played on a trumpet have a different quality about it from the same pitch played on a flute? The answer to these questions is the individual tone colour or timbre of each voice or instrument. A same pitch played on two different instruments sounds different because of the construction of the instrument. This also affects instruments of the same type. A cheap upright piano does not have the same quality in sound as an expensive Steinway concert grand!

Different tone colours

The oldest and most natural instrument used in making music is the human voice. It is the individual quality of each singing voice that adds to the success of a performance. The way a voice expresses emotion and conveys it to the audience makes some performers extremely popular. Voices are also joined together in choirs. A mixed choir using both male and female voices is divided into four voice parts: soprano, alto, tenor and bass. The sound produced by a mixed choir is entirely different from a purely male voice choir or choir consisting of only women's voices. Children's voices produce yet another different tone colour from adult voices.

The range of tone colours possible by using different combinations of musical instruments is impossible to explain in words. The modern symphony orchestra, for example, is arranged in sections of strings, woodwinds, brasses and percussion. The different tone qualities of individual instruments and combinations are easiest explained and learned by both listening to music and perhaps studying musical scores to see how the instruments are arranged.

Exercise 16.1 (Listening)

Listen to a demonstration of different tone colours.

Arrangement and orchestration

An arrangement involves adapting music for voices or instruments different from the original. Orchestration is the process of arranging or scoring music for a symphony orchestra. The following table lists the instruments by section and in the standard order they are written on an orchestral score. The number of wind and brass instruments is shown, but not actual number of stringed instruments. If an instrument is not included anywhere in the composition, it will not be listed on the first page. In the rest of the score, each page only includes the instruments actually playing at that time.

Picc	𝄞	Piccolo	
2 Fl	𝄞	Flutes	
2 Ob	𝄞	Oboes	
Eng Hrn	𝄞	English horn	*Woodwinds*
2 Clar	𝄞	Clarinets	
2 Bsns	𝄢	Bassoons	
C Bsn	𝄢	Contra bassoon	
4 Hrns	𝄞	Horns	
2 Tpts	𝄞	Trumpets	
2 Trbs	𝄡 tenor clef	Trombones	*Brass*
Tuba	𝄢		
Timp	F♯, C, G	3 timpani, each tuned to a different pitch	*Percussion*
Vl I	𝄞	Violins	
Vl II	𝄞		
Vla	𝄡 Alto clef	Violas	*Strings*
VC	𝄢	Cello	
DB	𝄢	Double bass	

The conductor

Many people question the need for a conductor. After all, he or she just seems to stand and wave a baton. In reality, a conductor has responsibilities ranging from selecting the music, leading the rehearsals and deciding how the music is to be interpreted. Even though each player has a written part, the orchestra needs someone to stop and start everyone together, give cues and lead the changes in loudness and speed. A conductor usually leads with a baton in the right hand and uses the left to indicate the expression. In vocal music, the conductor uses both hands and does not usually use a baton.

Conducting different time signatures

There are various patterns used to conduct both vocal and instrumental music. Some of the most common are found in Figure 16.1, with arrows showing the direction the conductor follows. Practise following the patterns. When the arrow points downwards, that is the downbeat. An arrow pointing upwards is the upbeat.

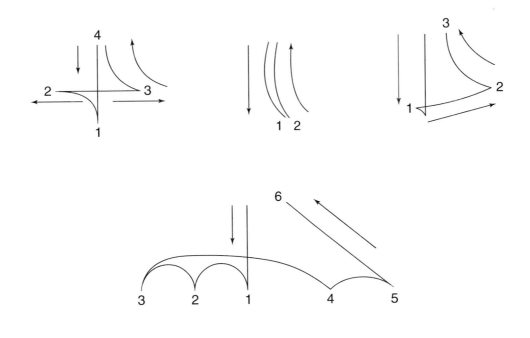

■ Figure 16.1

♫ᴄᴏᴍᴘᴀᴄᴛ **Exercise 16.2 (Practical)**

Turn on the CD and practise conducting the music provided.

Signs used to interpret music

You have seen how the way music is performed depends a lot on the artiste, the arrangement, interpretation and personal taste. The composer does, however, usually give some indications by using certain signs for the desired speed, dynamics and overall feeling.

Tempo

The speed of the music or tempo was touched on in Unit 1. The terms used, mainly English and Italian, only suggest how fast the music is meant to be. Many composers now use their native language, with German and French becoming more common.

The following list contains some of the terms used for indicating tempo. They are arranged from slow to fast, many of them meaning more or less the same thing. (A more complete list of Italian terms is located at the back of this book.)

> **Largo** = very slow. **Lento** = slow. **Grave** = slow and solemn. **Larghetto** = slightly faster than largo.
>
> **Adagio** = slow, but not as slow as largo. **Moderato** = medium speed. **Andante** = medium speed, walking pace.
>
> **Allegretto** = a little slower than allegro. **Allegro** = fast, cheerful, quick, merry. **Presto** = very fast, faster than allegro.

When an accurate speed is desired by the composer, a metronome marking may be found at the beginning of the composition. The metronome is an instrument that clicks at a set rate. A metronome marking looks like this: mm ♩ = 110. This means that in one minute, 110 crotchets beats will be counted.

Composers may not give a tempo indication, but instead use descriptive words to define the feeling of a work. Examples include **dolce** = sweetly; **grazioso** = gracefully; **amoroso** = loving; **giocoso** = playful.

Titles such as minuet, lullaby or blues also give a performer clues about the style of a composition. In such cases, however, it is up to the performer to know the characteristics of that style of music in order to perform it properly.

Changes in speed

Music does not always stay at the same speed throughout and changes add variety and sometimes drama. There are various signs and musical terms used to indicate changes of tempo. A few of the most common are:

> **Accelerando** (accel) = gradually increasing speed (think of pressing the accelerator on a car!).
>
> **Rallentando** (rall) = getting gradually slower.
>
> **Ritenuto** (rit) = getting slower.
>
> **A tempo** = go back to the original speed.

⌢ = pause. Known as the fermata sign, if written over an individual note it indicates that it is to be held longer than normal. It is up to the performer to decide on the length the note is held. In group playing, the conductor would direct the hold.

Dynamics

Most music is performed using different levels of loudness and softness, referred to as dynamics. Words or signs are written below the staff at the beginning of the piece, with new instructions given throughout. Some of the most common signs and abbreviations for dynamics are as follows: **piano** (p) = soft; **pianissimo** (pp) = very soft; **mezzo piano** (mp) = medium soft; **forte** (f) = loud; **fortissimo** (ff) = very loud; **mezzo forte** (mf) = medium loud; **sforzando** (sfz) = suddenly loud; **crescendo** (cres) = gradually becoming louder; **decrescendo/diminuendo** (dim) = gradually becoming softer. Signs for crescendo and diminuendo are ⊂ and ⊃ .

Articulation

Articulation is the way an individual note is performed. Some of the signs used are as follows:

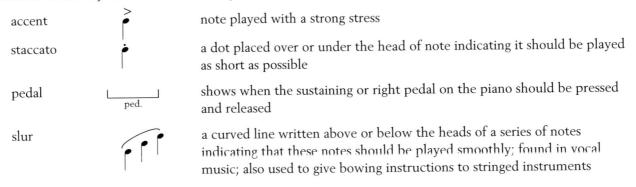

accent		note played with a strong stress
staccato		a dot placed over or under the head of note indicating it should be played as short as possible
pedal	ped.	shows when the sustaining or right pedal on the piano should be pressed and released
slur		a curved line written above or below the heads of a series of notes indicating that these notes should be played smoothly; found in vocal music; also used to give bowing instructions to stringed instruments

---

GOALS

1 Understand about tone colour or timbre.

2 Know the difference between an arrangement and orchestration.

3 Be able to conduct music in basic time signatures.

4 Know some of the words and signs that are used in interpreting music (speed, articulation, dynamics).

17

Ornaments and non-harmonic tones

Throughout the ages, most music has used embellishment and ornamentation to some degree. Many students, however, feel that the study of adding ornaments is only useful to those involved in learning older music such as the intricate compositions of J.S. Bach (1685–1750). This is not entirely true. Today's popular music, especially jazz for example, uses improvising to add colourful and creative embellishment. Improvising involves creating music while performing rather than playing a composition that is already completely written down.

One period of music, known as baroque, dating roughly from 1600–1750, does stand apart as a time when ornaments were used extensively. Being able to improvise decoration for a piece of music was a skill required by all musicians, especially solo performers. Composers did not always write out the entire music, but used symbols to indicate ornaments. The musicians were expected to know what to add from the symbols. Many composers of that period were virtuoso performers in their own right, so obviously knew how they wanted to ornament their own work without having to write it out in full. There is also a practical reason for the use of ornamentation in baroque music. Keyboard music was written for instruments such as the harpsichord and clavichord. Both instruments have a rather dry sound and no way of sustaining a held note. Adding embellishment to a note was a way of making it last longer. As time moved on, musical styles changed and composers notated their music differently. Most of the symbols and signs used a few hundred years ago are no longer seen in music. A few are still used, however, and we will look at each of these briefly. A more in-depth study would be necessary for anyone wanting to perform embellishments, as performance practices depend on the actual style of the music.

Ornaments

The trill

There are different ways of indicating a trill. Sometimes tr or 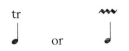 is used.

A trill involves quickly alternating between a written pitch and the note above it. Think of a bird trilling! The trill may begin on the written note, or the upper note and alternate downwards to the written note.

Unmeasured trills are to be performed as quickly as possible, obviously depending on the expertise of the performer. Other trills are measured more accurately. Performing a trill correctly largely depends on the style and period of the music.

Unmeasured trill

■ Figure 17.1

Measured trill

■ Figure 17.2

The turn

The turn is an ornament using four or perhaps five notes. There is a principal note which the other notes move or turn around. The sign for a turn is ∾. Sometimes a trill will finish by using a turn.

Symbol for turn

■ Figure 17.3

Example of a trill ending with a turn

■ Figure 17.4

Grace notes

A grace note is a very small printed note that is not counted in the general rhythm of the music. It is almost crushed into the note following it. However, in older music such as that of Bach or Mozart, the grace notes were played more evenly.

Examples of grace notes

■ Figure 17.5

Grace notes in older music

■ Figure 17.6

Mordent

The mordent consists of a written note quickly alternated with the note below it. The sign for a mordent is ❧.

■ Figure 17.7

The inverted mordent, notated as ❧, involves alternating between the written note and the note immediately above it.

■ Figure 17.8

Broken chords

A broken chord, also known as an arpeggio, is represented by a wavy vertical line. This indicates that the notes in the chord are to be played separately in succession, not simultaneously. Anyone strumming across the strings of a guitar is playing a broken chord!

Example of broken chord or arpeggio

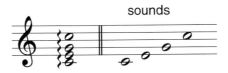

■ Figure 17.9

◎ Exercise 17.1 (Listening)

Listen to a demonstration of the ornaments you have studied.

Non-harmonic tones

Non-harmonic tones are different from ornaments in that they are actually written into a melody to add interest and feeling, but do not belong to the accompanying chord. These notes may be found in all styles of music. The most commonly used, the passing tone, neighbouring tone, suspension, anticipation and appoggiatura, will be explained and demonstrated.

Passing tones

The passing tone is approached by a step and is also followed by a step. It is usually found on a weak beat and is not sounded with a chord. In the first bar of the example, the overall harmony is that of C major. The notes used on each beat are C, E, G. These are the pitches of a C major triad. The F found on the second half of the second beat functions as a passing tone to join the E and G in the melody. In the second bar, the overall harmony is F major. The E and D are used as two consecutive passing tones to link the F and C.

Example using passing tones

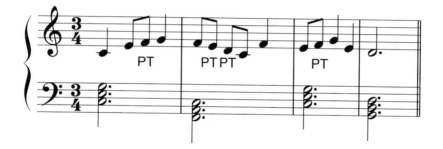

  Figure 17.10

Neighbouring tones

A neighbouring tone is used between two repeated notes in the melody. It is approached and left by movement of a step, either up or down, and may use either a semitone or tone. The example shows both upper and lower neighbouring tones and uses both semitones and tones.

Example using neighbouring tones

Figure 17.11

Suspension

The suspension is a note belonging to one chord that continues to sound through a change to a new harmony. The suspended note then moves down by step to resolve into a note belonging to the new chord. Using a suspension is a good way to create a feeling of tension which is then quickly resolved.

Example using suspensions

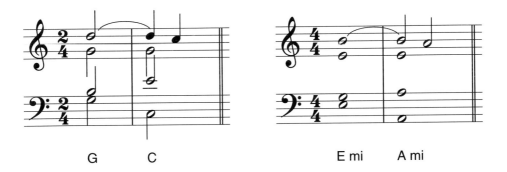

■ Figure 17.12

Anticipation

An anticipation is the opposite of the suspension. Instead of holding a note over into the new harmony, it anticipates a note from the new harmony before the chord is actually sounded. The anticipation is often found at the end of a piece.

Example showing anticipation

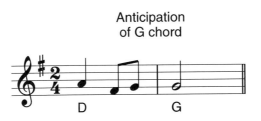

■ Figure 17.13

Appoggiatura

The appoggiatura is an accented non-harmonic tone. This means that the dissonance is sounded on a strong beat. The appoggiatura is approached by a skip in the melody and resolved by step in the opposite direction of the skip. The word is Italian, roughly meaning to lean. The non-harmonic note does not belong to the harmony and is leaning into the chord, creating a dissonance which must be resolved.

Example of the appoggiatura

■ Figure 17.14

Exercise 17.2 (Listening)

Listen to the examples of the different non-harmonic tones.

> **GOALS**
>
> 1 Understand the difference between ornaments and non-harmonic tones.
>
> 2 Know the basic notation for different ornaments.
>
> 3 Be able to recognize ornaments as they are played.
>
> 4 Know the basic notation of non-harmonic tones.
>
> 5 Be able to recognize non-harmonic tones when they are played.

18

Music theory in the 20th century and beyond

'Classical' music of the 20th century has developed in a variety of ways. The theory has incorporated a wide range of ideas from the past and combined them in new, innovative ways. There is more use of dissonance, new scales have been devised and rhythms are more irregular. This unit briefly explores some of the ways in which music theory has changed in more recent years.

Chords

During the past century, there has been much experimentation in building chords in new ways. Triads with added notes of the ninth, eleventh and thirteenth are found much more often. This causes the key or tonal centre to become vague. Chords are also built by using the interval of a fourth, not the third and the augmented fourth (tritone) is left unresolved. This adds more dissonance and blurring of the tonal centre. Other chords are also constructed of dissonant seconds, many written as clusters with all of the notes of a scale clustered together.

Exercise 18.1 (Listening)

Study the examples of chords constructed in various ways. Listen to a demonstration on the CD.

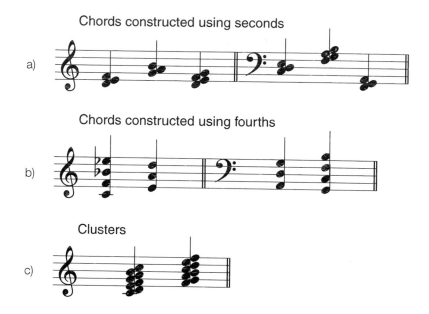

■ Figure 18.1

Atonality

Following World War I there was a period of intense experimentation with music theory. Composers such as Arnold Schoenberg worked at getting rid of traditional harmony, especially the tonal centre, by using a twelve tone row. Each composition is based on a series or row made of all twelve chromatic tones arranged in a specific order by the composer. The order of the row stays the same throughout the work, but may be varied by transposing it by octaves, changing the rhythm or using the row backwards. Because there is no tonal centre or key, each of the twelve chromatic tones being equal in status, this type of music is referred to as atonal.

Example of a twelve tone row

■ Figure 18.2

Exercise 18.2 (Listening)

Listen to a demonstration of the twelve tone row.

Other scales

Besides the use of the twelve tone row, composers also devised their own scales called synthetic scales. Two different scales may be found placed against one another in a sort of counterpoint. This creates two different tonal centres and is called polytonal music. Placing two different modes such as major or minor together creates polymodal music.

Examples of polytonal and polymodal music

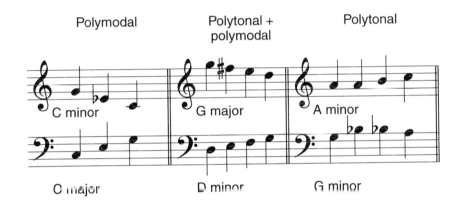

■ Figure 18.3

Exercise 18.3 (Listening)

Listen to a demonstration of polytonal and polymodal music.

The whole tone scale is built completely of whole tones and has only six notes in the octave. For example, the notes in the C octave are C, D, E, F♯, G♯, A♯ and C. This scale does not include the interval of the perfect fourth or perfect fifth and has no leading tone. Again, there is a loss of tonal feeling since all the tones in the scale are equal. The pentatonic scale has only five notes and is often found in the music of China and Africa. Different pentatonic scales have been used in 20th-century music, but the most common are C, D, E, G, A or C, D♭, E♭, G, A. The black keys of the piano keyboard form a pentatonic scale. Note that any pitch can be the starting point for these different scales, just as in major and minor scales.

Examples of whole tone and pentatonic scales

Whole tone scale

Pentatonic

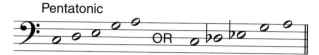

Exercise 18.4 (Written)

Construct a whole tone scale beginning on the following notes:

a)

b)

■ Figure 18.5

disc Exercise 18.5 (Listening)

Listen to a demonstration of whole tone and pentatonic scales.

Neoclassical ideas

Following the period of experimentation at the start of the 20th century, the 1920s saw a return to an interest in past styles and forms in music. Once again counterpoint was used in new compositions. These works, however, also combined some of the new innovations. The individual melody lines were written without regard for a single tonal centre. Elements from folk music were fused with more complex music. This is especially true in the music of the Hungarian composer, Bela Bartok. The influence of jazz which was developing in America can also be seen in works of this period.

Other innovations

During the second half of the 20th century, there was again more attempts in experimenting with sounds. One example is the 'prepared' piano used by the composer John Cage. He artificially altered the sound of a piano by inserting objects such as felt, paper, rubber wedges or metal into the strings. In France, a practice known as *musique concrete* used recordings of noises and everyday sounds as the basic material, not musical tones. These practices, however, were not mainstream.

The future

It is unclear what directions music theory will follow in the 21st century. All indications show that there will not only be further experimentation, but also interesting new uses of established practices. One composer, Mark-Anthony Turnage combines both contemporary classical music with modern jazz. There is no doubt that the possibilities for new musical creativity in the future are endless!

GOALS

1 Know some of the new ways chords were constructed in the 20th century.

2 Understand how a twelve tone row is constructed.

3 Define polytonal and polymodal.

4 Be able to construct a whole tone scale, starting on different pitches.

Answers

Exercise 18.4

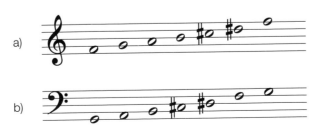

■ Figure 18.6

Taking it further

Listed below are suggestions for further study of music theory and related musical activities:

The Associated Board of the Royal Schools of Music
14 Bedford Square
London WC1B 3JG
United Kingdom

www.abrsm.publishing.co.uk

The Associated Board provides graded music for a wide variety of instruments and voice. They also have published a music theory textbook, *The AB Guide to Music Theory* and graded music theory workbooks. The emphasis is mainly classical, although some jazz has recently been introduced.

For students interested in applying music theory to piano or electronic keyboard, *The Complete Piano Player* and *The Complete Keyboard Player* are useful books. These are written by Kenneth Baker and published by Wise Publications.

Advice on finding a private music teacher:
- Recommendation by word of mouth.
- Some public libraries keep lists of local teachers.
- Check adverts in local newspapers.
- Contact local college or universities. Many advanced music students offer individual lessons.

Opportunities for group learning:
- Many adult education centres and local colleges offer various day or evening classes in music.
- Local groups such as choruses or brass bands often provide free instruction in reading and performing music.

The British and International Music Yearbook published by Rhinegold, is an extensive directory containing information on education, music venues and music book publishers.

Rhinegold Publishing Ltd.
241 Shaftesbury Avenue
London WC2H 8EH

www.rhinegold.co.uk/music on the web

There are many websites which sell music books and sheet music of all types. A few are listed below:

www.musicexchange

www.sheetmusicdirect.com

www.musicroom.com

www.sheetmusicplus.com

www.lookmusic.com

Glossary

Musical terms used in this book

accent   special stress or emphasis given to a note

accidental   symbol written as needed before a pitch to raise or lower it

accompaniment   musical background added to the main melody

alto   second highest voice in four-part chorale writing; a low female voice

alto clef   clef using the third line of a staff as middle C; mainly used for notating music for viola

arrangement   music adapted for performance in a different way from how it was originally written

augment   make larger; applies to intervals and chords

bar (measure)   space between two bar-lines

bar-line   vertical line dividing written music into bars, each containing the number of beats shown by the time signature

bass   lowest male voice in four-part chorale writing

bass clef   see **F clef**

beam   used in place of flags to group notes together

beat   underlying pulse of each bar which is counted

brace   bracket joining two or more staves together

breve   note held twice as long as a semibreve (not often used in modern notation)

C clef   clef used to locate middle C on either the third or fourth lines of a staff

cadence   chord progression found at the end of a phrase, section or entire work

chord   three or more pitches played or sung together

chord symbol   letter-name representing a chord, written above a melody line to show the chord accompaniment

clef   sign placed at the beginning of a work to indicate a certain pitch, usually middle C

coda   extra bars added to the end of a composition

common time $\frac{4}{4}$ time, sometimes abbreviated as C instead of the numbers

compound interval   interval larger than an octave

compound time   time signature where each beat of the bar is divided by three (♪ ♪ ♪)

counterpoint   melodies written against one another; linear music

crotchet (quarter note)   note receiving one-quarter of a semibreve

degrees   individual notes of a scale

diminish   make smaller; applies to intervals and chords

dotted note   note receiving half the value again of its original length

double bar-lines   vertical lines marking the end of a work or section of a large composition

double flat   sign which lowers an already flattened note

doubled sharp   sign which raises an already sharpened note

duet   music for two performers

dynamics   varying loudness and softness in music

eighth note   see **quaver**

F clef   clef marking the fourth line as the F below middle C; also known as bass clef

fine   end of a work, the finish

flat   sign which lowers the pitch of a note by one semitone

G clef   clef marking the second line as G above middle C; also known as treble clef

grace note   ornamental note of short duration

half note   see **minim**

half tone   see **semitone**

harmony   study of combinations of pitches, mainly chords

interval   distance or space between two pitches

inversion   change in the order of notes

key   tonal centre based on a scale; also, a lever depressed on a keyboard

keynote first note of a scale

key signature sharps or flats shown on the staff at the beginning of a work or section of a work

leger (ledger) **line** short line added above or below the staff as needed

measure see **bar**

melody organized series of pitches

meter basic scheme of beats; same as time signature

metronome machine which beats time at a set pulse

middle C first leger line both below the treble staff and above the bass staff; also, the C nearest the middle of the keyboard

minim (half note) note receiving half the value of a semibreve

natural sign cancels a sharp or flat

notation writing music down

note symbol used to show the length and pitch of musical sounds

octave interval consisting of the eight notes of any scale, covering the distance between one note and the next one higher or lower with the same letter-name

ornament embellishment added to music, usually to the melody line

phrase section of music, similar to a sentence in language

pitch highness or lowness of a musical sound

quarter note see **crotchet**

quaver (eighth note) note receiving half the value of a crotchet

repeat sign sign consisting of vertical double lines and matching dots showing that the music in between is to be repeated

rest symbol indicating periods of silence

rhythm notes of various duration organized into patterns to fit a time signature

scale series of alphabetically arranged pitches

score written music showing all the parts for various instruments and voices on one page

semibreve (whole note) note with the longest duration found in most modern music notation

semiquaver (sixteenth note) note receiving half the value of a quaver

semitone (half tone) smallest interval in music notation

sharp sign raising a pitch one semitone

simple time   time signature where each beat of the bar is divided by 2 ($\frac{2}{4}$)

sixteenth note   see **semiquaver**

slur   curved line drawn above the heads of two or more consecutive notes to show they should be played smoothly

solo   (for) one performer only

soprano   highest female voice in four-part vocal writing

staccato   detached, short

staff (stave)   five lines and four spaces on which music is notated

syncopation   displaced accents put on normally weak beats

tempo   speed of a piece of music

tenor   highest male voice in four-part vocal writing

tenor clef   C clef placing middle C on the fourth line of the staff

tie   curved line joining two notes of the same pitch, adding length to the duration of the original note

time signature   two numbers or a sign placed at the beginning of music, the top number showing the number of beats in each bar, the bottom number giving the value of the note receiving one beat

tone (whole tone)   interval made of two semitones; also a musical sound with a definite pitch

tonic   first degree of a scale

transposing   to write or perform music in a different key or octave from which it was originally written

treble clef   see **G clef**

triad   chord containing three notes

trill   ornament performed by quick alternation between the given note and the note either above or below it

triplet   group of notes which takes the place of two of the same kind (i.e. two quavers); notated by a 3 and a bracket

tritone   dissonant interval of the augmented fourth/diminished fifth

unison   two notes having the same letter-name

waltz   dance written in $\frac{3}{4}$ time

whole note   see **semibreve**

Italian terms commonly used in music

a cappella   unaccompanied voices

accelerando   gradually becoming faster

adagio   leisurely, slow tempo

agitato   excited, agitated

allegretto   lively tempo, not as fast as allegro

allegro   cheerful, rapid tempo

andante   moderate, walking speed

andantino   slightly faster than **andante**

animato   animated, with spirit

assai   very

a tempo   return to the original speed

brio   brilliance, spirit

cantabile   in a singing style

con   with

crescendo   gradually increasing in loudness

descrescendo   gradually becoming softer

diminuendo   gradually becoming softer

dolce   sweetly

expressivo   with expression

forte   (f) loud

forte piano   loud, then suddenly soft

fortissimo   (ff) very loud

giocoso   playful

grave   slow, solemn

grazioso   gracefully

largetto   slow but not as slow as **largo**

largo   slow, stately tempo, slower than **lento**

legato   smooth and connected manner of playing or singing

lento   slow but not as slow as **largo**

maestoso majestically

marcato marked, accented

meno less

moderate at a moderate speed

molto very

moto motion

non not

pesante heavy

piano (p) soft

piu more

poco little

presto very fast

prestissimo as quickly as possible

prima, primo first

quasi similar to

rallentando gradually becoming slower

ritardando growing slower

rubato with freedom in the rhythm

scherzando playful

semplice simply

sempre always

senza without

simile the same

sostenuto sustained

subeto suddenly

tranquillo quiet

vivace quick, lively tempo

vivo lively

Note that some of the words, such as **con** (with) or **senza** (without), are combined to give instructions to the performer.

Note values

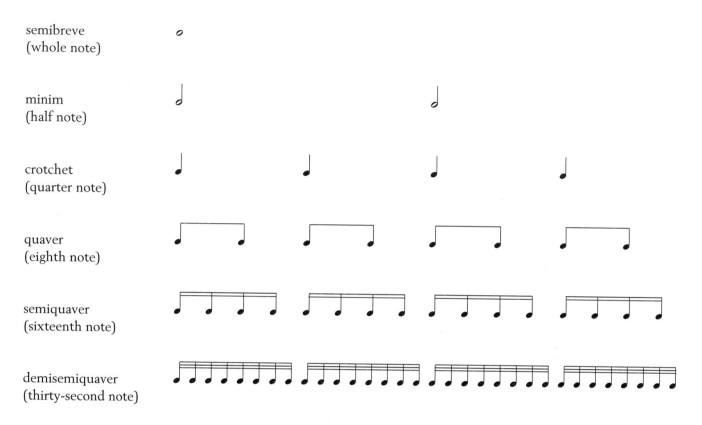

semibreve
(whole note)

minim
(half note)

crotchet
(quarter note)

quaver
(eighth note)

semiquaver
(sixteenth note)

demisemiquaver
(thirty-second note)

Rests

—	semibreve (whole note)
—	minim (half note)
𝄽	crotchet (quarter note)
𝄾	quaver (eighth note)
𝄿	semiquaver (sixteenth note)
𝅀	demisemiquaver (thirty-second note)

Table of key signatures

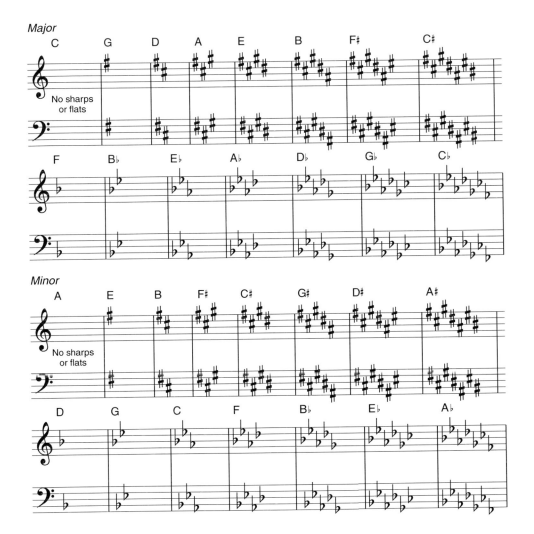

Notes on the staff

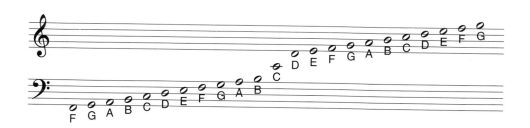